GREAT CHEFS of New Orleans II

Other Avon Books
GREAT CHEFS OF SAN FRANCISCO

GREAT CHEFS of New Orleans II

AVON
PUBLISHERS OF BARD, CAMELOT, DISCUS AND FLARE BOOKS

THE GREAT CHEFS™ OF NEW ORLEANS II is an original
publication of Avon Books. This work has never before
appeared in book form.

AVON BOOKS
A division of
The Hearst Corporation
1790 Broadway
New York, New York 10019

First Avon Printing, August, 1984

AVON TRADEMARK REG. U.S. PAT. OFF. AND IN
OTHER COUNTRIES, MARCA REGISTRADA, HECHO EN
U.S.A.

Printed in the U.S.A.

DON 10 9 8 7 6 5 4 3 2 1

New Orleans is a city profoundly influenced by the French way of life and this is clearly evident in most of the restaurants featured in the Great Chefs television series and in this book. Many of the Great Chefs were trained in France and you can see how they have adapted their French cooking skills to match the style of the new American cuisine.

The Great Chefs work by culinary instinct. The ultimate test is in the tasting, so do as the chefs do. Taste a dish and, if it requires something, add it. If it is good, leave it alone— for knowing when to quit is equally important. Above all, allow yourself the sensual pleasure of working with the best and most beautiful foods in the creation of dishes that will be delightful to share with your family and friends.

One note regarding the recipes: The number of servings and the preparation time are listed for each dish. Certain recipes also include the phrase *note elapsed time*. This indicates that advance preparation is needed. Always read the entire recipe before planning your dinner.

GREAT CHEFS OF NEW ORLEANS II represents thirteen master cooking classes featuring outstanding chefs from the New Orleans metropolitan area. Each program includes the preparation and presentation of a complete menu. The series was designed both to instruct the home cook in a wide range of cooking techniques and to provide the rare opportunity to observe working chefs practicing their art in their own kitchens. GREAT CHEFS OF NEW ORLEANS II includes many of the same chefs as the first New Orleans book, but with all new menus and recipes.

CONTENTS

✗

CONTENTS

CHEF WARREN LE RUTH
LE RUTH'S

Warren Le Ruth is a great chef and a great American raconteur! He roars with laughter as he spins tales of growing up in New Orleans during the depression. "We always sat in the kitchen around a big table; the family gathered there, for meals, for talking, and I did my schoolwork in that kitchen," he says fondly. "My mother was a wonderful baker and candy maker so it just seemed natural for me to get a job in a bakery."

There is nothing like an American success story and Warren, without the basic training of the European-born chefs, just kept working and studying, becoming the first in his family to go to college since the Civil War. "I loved math and physics," he says, "And I loved cooking so it seemed like a fine combination to put it all together for the future." As a member of the Louisiana National Guard, Warren completed cook and baker's school, mess steward's school and food supervisor's school so that he could get a job as baker in some of the fine hotels of New Orleans.

"I got drafted during the Korean War," he says, "I was personal chef to General Clark in Korea. Those generals liked everything in the grand southern manner; we used to fill six trucks with dining paraphanalia to feed thirteen men!" With visions of M*A*S*H in mind, it would seem that young Warren's future career as master chef was won on the battlegrounds of Korea. Unlike the young Europeans, who spent their boyhood in apprenticeships to hotel chefs, Le Ruth went directly to work for Proctor & Gamble upon his army discharge. In their research division, he helped develop the Duncan Hines cake mixes; from there he took other jobs, always involved with food and its tastes.

In 1966, Warren opened his Victorian-styled restaurant in Gretna, on the west bank of New Orleans. With typical ebullience he announced that his was the only restaurant in the New Orleans area to bake its own french bread daily and make its own French vanilla ice cream, high in butterfat, scented with Warren's own marinated vanilla beans. "Bread should be two hours old," he said, "not twelve." Who would disagree? Certainly not the customers and Le Ruth's had a waiting list of two weeks.

Le Ruth's menu is amazing in its virtuosity, different from New Orleans' typical French restaurants. The Potage Le Ruth, a rich, complex blend of oysters and "lots of artichoke hearts" has been imitated but Warren says his secret recipes are in a bank vault.

The two new secrets in the kitchen are Warren's sons Larry, 26 and Lee, 24. They have taken over for dad; the kitchen is theirs and the tall white toques fit easily.

They earned them, spending the past ten years side-by-side with their father in the kitchen, learning and creating. Larry studied at the Culinary Institute of America; Lee went to Paris to study in the kitchens of La Marée and Prunier's. Of course, the famous Le Ruth's menu is still intact but the brothers' have created some new dishes that "even the old man never thought of."

Warren Le Ruth and his sons have fine-tuned their famous restaurant, keeping the favorites, adding new treasures. Warren says, "I have neither the time nor the inclination to bother with the past, because the future is already in place." ⚡

LE RUTH'S
GRETNA

MENU

OYSTERS BELLE RIVE
An oyster appetizer inspired by the flavorful cuisine of the French Riviera

REDFISH À LA TERMEREAU
A seafood specialty combining redfish and lobster created especially for Le Ruth's

CASSATA PARFAIT TORTE
A frozen chocolate sponge cake and whipped cream confection

✗

Oysters Belle Rive

SERVINGS: 10–12
PREPARATION TIME: 1 HOUR

GARLIC BUTTER
  2 cups soft butter
  2 cups soft margarine
  2 teaspoons salt
  2 teaspoons white pepper
  ⅓ cup olive oil
  ¼ cup white wine
  ¼ cup parsley, chopped
  ½ cup onion, chopped
10 garlic cloves, finely chopped

Whip butter and margarine with mixer until smooth. Add salt, white pepper, olive oil and wine to butter mixture and blend. Add parsley, onions and garlic and mix on high speed, scraping down sides occasionally, until butter turns white, about 10 minutes. Refrigerate.

(continued)

VIENNE SAUCE

- 4 cups cream
- 1 bunch green onions, chopped
- 4 large mushrooms, sliced
- ½ cup butter
- ½ teaspoon salt
- ¼ teaspoon white pepper
- ¼ teaspoon cayenne pepper
- ¼ cup white wine
- 1 egg yolk

Reduce cream by one-third. Sauté green onions and mushrooms in butter, then season with salt, white pepper and cayenne pepper. Cook mixture about 10 minutes over high heat, stirring regularly. Add white wine and reduced cream and bring to a boil. Remove from heat and allow to cool briefly. Whisk in yolk and bring back to a boil, stirring constantly. Remove immediately from heat and reserve.

ARTICHOKE SAUCE

- 20 artichoke hearts, sliced
- 4 garlic cloves, finely chopped
- 2 cups water
- ½ cup olive oil
- 4 bay leaves
- ½ tablespoon thyme
- ½ tablespoon salt
- ¼ teaspoon white pepper
- ¼ teaspoon black pepper
- ¼ teaspoon cayenne pepper
- 1 cup bread crumbs
- 1 cup Romano cheese

Place water, olive oil and seasonings in a large saucepan. Add artichokes and garlic and bring to a rolling boil. Stir in bread crumbs and cheese and heat thoroughly. Reserve.

ASSEMBLY

- 6 dozen oysters, shucked, allowing 6 each per person
- 36 oven-proof ramekins

First, reheat each of the sauces. Then, for each person, place 2 oysters each in the bottoms of 3 small ramekins. Fill one ramekin to the top with Garlic Butter, one with Vienne Sauce and one with Artichoke Sauce. Bake ramekins for 10 minutes at 400 degrees. Serve immediately.

REDFISH À LA
TERMEREAU

4 redfish fillets, about 5–6 ounces
  each
4 small rock lobster tails, removed
  from shell (large peeled shrimp may
  be substituted)
½ small onion, chopped
2 bay leaves
¼ teaspoon thyme
½ tomato, thinly sliced
½ cup white wine
1 cup fish stock (or combination of
  clam juice and white wine)
1 cup butter
1½ cups whipping cream
juice of ¼ lemon
cayenne pepper to taste
salt and white pepper to taste

Roll fillets around the lobster tails and place in buttered 8-inch square baking dish. Add onions, bay leaves, thyme, salt and white pepper. Top each fillet with a slice of tomato. Pour white wine and fish stock into pan with fillets. Melt and drizzle ½ cup butter over fish. Cover pan with foil and bake 15–20 minutes in 400-degree oven. Remove fish from pan and keep warm until serving. Drain fish drippings into a sauté pan and reduce by 90%. Pour whipping cream into another pan and reduce by 40%. Heat ½ cup butter until very hot. Add reduced cream to reduced fish drippings, then whip in hot butter. Add lemon juice and season to taste with cayenne, salt and pepper.

Spoon sauce over stuffed fillets and serve immediately.

SERVINGS: MAKES 4 9-INCH CAKES, EACH CAKE SERVES 10
PREPARATION TIME: 2 HOURS

CHOCOLATE GENOISE

7 eggs
⅔ cup sugar
½ cup flour
4 tablespoons cocoa
3 tablespoons cornstarch
2 teaspoons grated lemon rind

In a bowl, mix eggs and sugar. Heat over hot water, stirring constantly, to 110 degrees. Take off heat and whip 8–12 minutes on high speed with an electric mixer until very light and fluffy. Sift flour, cornstarch and cocoa together 3 times. Carefully fold the flour mixture and lemon rind into the egg mixture. Pour into 2 greased and floured 9-inch cake pans. Bake at 350 degrees until set and springy, about 25–30 minutes. Remove from oven, invert cakes and cool on racks.

PARFAIT FILLING

3 cups whipping cream
9 egg yolks
¾ cup powdered sugar
2 teaspoons vanilla
1 teaspoon grated lemon rind

Whip cream to stiff peaks and refrigerate until use. Whip yolks, sugar and vanilla for 7–9 minutes on high speed until very light. Add lemon rind. Gently fold egg yolk mixture into whipped cream.

ASSEMBLY

¼ cup glacéed (candied) fruit, diced
¼ cup maraschino cherries, chopped

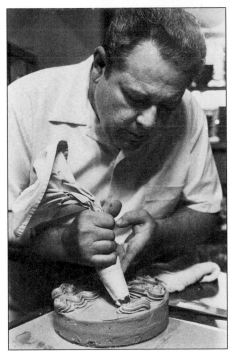

First cut waxed paper into 4 circles (9 inches in diameter) and place in the bottoms of 4 9-inch cake pans. Spoon filling evenly into cake pans, just enough to cover the bottoms. Sprinkle glacéed fruit and cherries on top of the filling. Spoon the remainder of the filling over fruit. Split both baked cakes horizontally and place one split cake layer on top of the filling in each pan. Freeze overnight. Unmold so that the cake layer will be on the bottom and peel off the waxed paper. Decorate the tops of the cakes with piped whipped cream and whole maraschino cherries. Keep frozen until serving time.

CHEF DANIEL BONNOT
RESTAURANT DE LA TOUR EIFFEL

With a typically French gesture of flicking away any problems in transporting the complete restaurant in the Eiffel Tower from Paris to New Orleans, Daniel Bonnot simply says, "It was in eleven-hundred pieces held together with thirty-thousand metric screws. It took twenty-one days to disassemble, so that we could carefully reconstruct it on St. Charles Avenue. Naturally, it is called the Restaurant de la Tour Eiffel."

Daniel, who, at the age of 14, made his own decision to attend and graduate from one of Paris' most difficult culinary academys, is adamant in his belief that the proper training of a great chef can be achieved in only one way. "The principles of cooking come first, at school," he says, "the learning part started with my apprenticeship. There is an evolution in learning the proper way to cook and it takes years, working for tough chefs." Daniel says, as he remembers the difficult conditions and the long hours of his apprenticeship. "We were always looking for perfection in making the classic French dishes and I believed that creating a new recipe was simply an excuse for not knowing the classics."

With such a strong, rather rigid set of standards, and an introduction to Alain Martin, chef at l'Auberge de la Vielle Tour in Guadaloupe, the 23-year old Daniel was confronted with the exotic tropical plumage of a new country and a new cuisine. "It was my first experience with Creole food and I couldn't believe the fish and vegetables and fruit—the fresh spices and herbs that were available," he recalled. "After three years I wanted to go to the U.S. and particularly to New Orleans because it seemed very French."

In 1971, at the age of 26, Daniel became the chef at Louis XVI in New Orleans. "It was everything I dreamed," he says. "It was the first new, classic French restaurant in New Orleans. My menu had Beef Wellington, racks of lamb with fresh vegetables, Maine lobsters in Sauce Americaine. The customers hadn't eaten these dishes outside of trips to France and the place was an overnight success."

With exceptional energy and in addition to his job as the chef, Daniel managed in the next ten years to open a patisserie, become a Professor of Cuisine at Tulane University, win two "Premier" bronze medals at New Orleans famed Food Festivals, become Editor of La Gazette Culinaire of New Orleans, Vice President of the Society of Chefs, an Honorary Citizen of New Orleans, Chef of the Year for 1980 and 1981 and, to top it all, honorary Captain of the New Orleans Police Department.

Now, for Daniel Bonnot, comes the Restaurant de la Tour Eiffel and a new way of cooking. "My way of thinking has changed; I was more conservative ten years ago," Daniel says. "The publics' tastes have changed; people travel, they have learned about cooking and wines; they are very sophisticated. There is a whole new generation of people who have great style and I want to combine the best of what I know with that style. The food is what I call Cuisine Gourmande—a little classic, a little country, a little nouvelle. It is my conception of the best of French food combined with New Orleans-American, and it is very exciting."

It is exciting for this young chef, who knew exactly what he wanted at the age of 14 and is now sitting in his own Eiffel Tower. Bon chance, Daniel Bonnot! ✗

RESTAURANT DE LA TOUR EIFFEL
NEW ORLEANS

MENU

CRAWFISH BEIGNETS
A spicy Caribbean appetizer

DUCK CONFIT
Duck poached in herbs and rendered fat

POTATOES SARLADAISE
Sautéed potatoes flavored with truffles

PEAR FLAN
Poached pears and custard cream in a tart shell

🏃

SERVINGS: 4–6 (28 BEIGNETS)
PREPARATION TIME: 30 MINUTES (NOTE ELAPSED TIME)

1 cup flour
1 teaspoon baking powder
1 cup water
1 teaspoon garlic, chopped
1 pimiento, chopped
3 green onions, chopped
4 drops Tabasco sauce
pinch of salt
8 ounces cooked crawfish tails, roughly
  chopped (cooked shrimp may be
  substituted)

In a bowl, mix ingredients in order listed. Cover bowl with damp towel and set aside for 30 minutes.

Drop by spoonfuls into 325-degree oil and fry until golden brown, about 7–8 minutes. Drain and serve hot with a lemon wedge.

SERVINGS: 4
PREPARATION TIME: 2 HOURS (NOTE ELAPSED TIME)

1 4–5 pound duck cut into 4 pieces
  (2 breasts, 2 legs)
1 pound tinned goose fat (available in
  specialty shops) plus rendered fat from
  duck
4 tablespoons coarse salt
2 tablespoons cracked black pepper
2 tablespoons fresh thyme, chopped
7 bay leaves
3 cloves garlic, chopped
1 sprig thyme

Combine salt, pepper, chopped thyme, 5 crumbled bay leaves, and 2 cloves chopped garlic and divide equally among 4 pieces of duck, pressing mixture onto both sides of each piece. Cover with plastic and refrigerate overnight.

In heavy saucepan over low heat, warm goose and duck fat just until melted. With a damp cloth, wipe seasoning from duck pieces and lay them skin side down in another saucepan. Cover completely with melted fat. Add 2 whole bay leaves, 1 clove chopped garlic, and 1 sprig thyme. Cook very slowly on top of the stove for 60–75 minutes until tender. Do not let fat boil.

Remove duck from fat and serve hot with Potatoes Sarladaise. The duck may be stored covered in strained fat in the refrigerator for up to a week.

POTATOES SARLADAISE

3 medium potatoes
1 serving spoon duck fat
1 truffle, sliced (one large wild
    mushroom may be substituted)
1 tablespoon fresh parsley, chopped
salt and pepper to taste

Peel and slice potatoes ⅛-inch thick. Pat dry and sauté in hot duck fat on top of the stove for about 20 minutes. At the last minute, remove from heat, toss with truffles and season with parsley, salt and pepper. Serve hot with Duck Confit.

PEAR FLAN

PASTRY DOUGH
 1 cup flour
 2 tablespoons sugar
pinch of salt
½ cup butter
½ cup water
 2 cups dried beans

Sift flour, sugar and salt together. Cut butter into small squares and work into flour mixture with fingers to form a coarse meal. Make a well in the center of the mixture and add water. Mix together to form a smooth paste. Form a ball and wrap in a damp towel. Refrigerate about half an hour. Roll out dough to fit a 9″ tart pan. Place dough in pan and prick bottom with a fork. Cover sides and bottom of dough with parchment paper and fill pan with beans. Bake for 20 minutes at 375 degrees. Remove parchment paper and beans. (Note: beans may be saved and reused for future baking.)

POACHED PEARS
 3 ripe pears, peeled
½ cup sugar
 2 cups water
peel from 1 lemon
 4 drops vanilla

Cover pears with remaining ingredients and simmer until easily pierced with a knife (approximately 15–20 minutes). Reserve liquid for use in custard cream.

Pear Flan

CUSTARD CREAM PASTRY FILLING
- *1 cup sugar*
- *2 whole eggs*
- *3 egg yolks*
- *2 tablespoons pear brandy (optional)*
- *3 tablespoons pear poaching liquid*
- *¼ cup flour*
- *1½ cups milk, scalded with 1 teaspoon vanilla*

ASSEMBLY
- *2–3 tablespoons ground, blanched almonds*

Whisk sugar, whole eggs, and 2 egg yolks in a bowl until thick and lemon-colored. Whisk in pear brandy and pear poaching liquid.

Add flour and beat until smooth. Beat in ½ cup hot milk, then add mixture to remaining milk. Stir over low heat just to boiling. Mixture will thicken very fast. Remove from heat, then pour into a bowl and let cool. When cool, beat in remaining yolk.

Cut pears in half lengthwise, remove core and stem, then slice ¼-inch thick from end to end. Spread pastry cream evenly on bottom of baked tart shell and arrange sliced pears in spoke pattern on top of the cream. Fill tart to top with remaining cream. Sprinkle with almonds and bake at 325 degrees for 45 minutes. Serve warm or cold.

CHEF WILLY COLN
WILLY COLN'S RESTAURANT

Willy Coln's menu looks Continental-Classic at first glance, then the eye picks up some lovely subtleties in the short descriptions under each offering. A talk with the chef brings out his philosophies as well as his extraordinary background and love of cooking.

"I create my menu, taking the classics a bit farther than I was taught as a boy, adding dishes that are not on other menus, tasting always and using spices with great care," the soft-spoken Willy says. "I like to add special appetizers and main courses to my menu because my customers expect to find a few surprises and it gives me great pleasure."

One little surprise is an appetizer of seviche, that classic melange of absolutely fresh, firm white fish, traditionally marinated in lime juice, onions and a bit of olive oil. Willy takes it to its maximum, using not only tender redfish but adding fresh shrimp and pearly scallops, lime and lemon juices, tomato, bell peppers, garlic,

16

thyme, cloves, Worcestershire sauce and, for a zing, a red hot pepper. The result is a marvelous mix of flavors and textures. "My local customers wouldn't touch my seviche for a long time because it was odd and too new for them but I kept it on the menu and now half of them order it when they come to dinner," Willy says.

Willy Coln's Restaurant, in Gretna, is a charming little Bavarian chalet complete with stone fireplace, soft lighting, terra cotta colored tablecloths and racks of green glass wine bottles used to separate the cozy dining rooms. His kitchen, built to specifications, of stainless steel and tile, is the perfect home to this master chef.

Willy was born in Cologne, Germany in 1940 and apprenticed to a fine chef at the age of 14. The work was desperately hard—12-hour days of learning with no pay. He saw the world from the galley kitchens of the Holland-American line, the kitchen windows of the Carlton in London, and the peephole windows of the boarding houses in Zurich and Basel, where the boy worked in hotel kitchens. In 1967, Willy came to America. "I liked the freedom of this country," he says. "There were no visas; there was a chance to be creative, to be involved in menus, with the food."

Willy and his wife, Erna, bought their restaurant on the west bank of New Orleans in 1976. The menu of ravishing dishes is quite Willy Coln's own creation. His Escargots Normande combines diced shallots, mushrooms, spices and Calvados with the snail butter, served piping hot over tiny escargots; the buttery smoked salmon with capers, onions and sour cream also stars a golden, crisp potato pancake, for texture. A steaming casserole of plump oysters is sauced with hot cream and melting Gruyere cheese. One of the great favorites is the Jäger Schnitzel, milk-fed Wisconsin veal simmered in a pale,

light cream sauce with chanterelles and fresh mushrooms; another is the roasted Duckling Madagascar, the duck in a tangy green peppercorn sauce served with Willy's own red cabbage, cooked gently in duck stock and a mirepoix of vegetables. His guests love Willy's roasted veal shank for two with vegetables. It seems that Willy can do no wrong for his customers; he makes Bouilliabaisse; Veal Piccata Milanese with his special tomato sauce garnished with julienned strips of ham and mushrooms, served with homemade fettuccine, and, in season, soft-shelled crabs sautéed in lemon-butter with crabmeat and artichokes.

And so, Willy Coln is very much at home in his kitchen. He serves the very best to his customers but he still says, "It is very important for my guests to tell me if something is right—or wrong. No matter what, I welcome their comments." ✗

WILLY COLN'S
GRETNA

MENU

COLD POACHED SALMON WITH SAUCE VERTE
Salmon poached with herbs and wine, topped with green mayonnaise

BAHAMIAN CHOWDER
A hearty seafood and vegetable soup garnished with grated cheese

DUCK IN GREEN PEPPERCORN SAUCE
Roast duck served with braised red cabbage

STRAWBERRIES ROMANOFF
Marinated strawberries with whipped cream

SERVINGS: 4
PREPARATION TIME: 30 minutes

SAUCE VERTE

2 ounces fresh spinach
2 tablespoons fresh parsley
2 teaspoons fresh tarragon
1 cup mayonnaise

POACHED SALMON

*1 2-pound salmon, filleted (leave
   skin on)*
1 cup Chablis wine
1 cup cold water
1 lemon, sliced
1 carrot, sliced
½ onion, sliced
4 bay leaves
2 sprigs parsley
1 teaspoon thyme
½ teaspoon salt
½ teaspoon black peppercorns, crushed
½ cucumber, sliced (garnish)
lemon, sliced (garnish)

Blanch spinach, parsley and tarragon. Chop fine and squeeze in a
towel to remove as much liquid as
possible. Combine all ingredients in
a mixing bowl and reserve.

Place salmon, skin side up, in an
oven-proof casserole dish. Add
Chablis wine, water, lemon, carrot,
onion, bay leaves, parsley, thyme,
salt and crushed peppercorns.
Cover casserole tightly and poach in
a 400-degree oven for 20 minutes.
Cool poached salmon in cooking liquid and chill thoroughly. Remove
skin of salmon, then slice salmon
into 1¼-inch wide pieces. To serve,
garnish salmon with Sauce Verte,
and cucumber and lemon slices.

4 ounces raw shrimp, peeled and
deveined
4 ounces fresh fish, boneless, skinless
and diced
1 medium carrot, julienned
1 small green pepper, julienned
2 green onions, julienned
1 medium onion, julienned
1 stalk celery, julienned
2 tablespoons olive oil
1 large bay leaf
1 medium clove garlic, minced
½ teaspoon dried thyme leaves
⅛ teaspoon cayenne pepper
¼ teaspoon black pepper
¼ teaspoon salt
2 tablespoons tomato paste
2 tablespoons flour
2 medium tomatoes, peeled and
julienned
½ cup dry white wine
1 tablespoon parsley leaves and stems,
finely chopped
1½ quarts fish stock
grated Gruyère cheese to garnish

Sauté the shrimp, fish, carrot, green pepper, green onion, onion and celery in the hot oil for 2 minutes. Add the bay leaf, garlic, seasonings and tomato paste. Dust the mixture with the flour. Stir the mixture until the flour is blended. Add the tomatoes, white wine, parsley and fish stock. Adjust seasoning, then bring to a boil. Reduce heat and simmer for 5 minutes. To serve, grate Gruyère cheese on top of individual bowls of chowder.

Duck in Green Peppercorn Sauce

SERVINGS: 4
PREPARATION TIME: 1½ HOURS (NOTE ELAPSED TIME)

2 4–5 pound ducks
1 onion, roughly chopped
1 stalk celery, roughly chopped
1 carrot, roughly chopped
1 cup dry red wine
2 cups chicken stock or chicken bouillon
2 teaspoons sage
2 teaspoons savory
1 tablespoon green peppercorns
1 tablespoon butter
2 teaspoons arrowroot dissolved in
   ½ cup water
salt and pepper to taste

Remove neck, neck skin, wings and gizzard from ducks and reserve for sauce. Wash ducks and pat dry. Salt and pepper ducks inside and out. Brown ducks on a rack placed in a deep roasting pan for 45 minutes in a 400-degree oven. Reduce heat to 325 degrees and cook until done, about 45 minutes, basting ducks twice with drippings. Split cooked ducks in half along the back bone. Remove and reserve all bones for sauce and set boned duck halves aside. Reserve 2 tablespoons of fat from drippings in roasting pan. In a large saucepan, on top of the stove, brown neck, neck skin, wings,

(continued)

DUCK IN GREEN
PEPPERCORN SAUCE

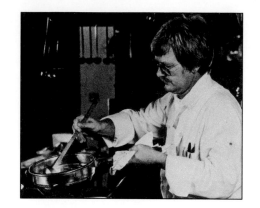

gizzard and bones with onions, celery and carrots in duck fat. Add red wine, chicken stock, sage and savory. Reduce broth to approximately 2 cups and strain. Toss green peppercorns in melted butter in a sauté pan. Add reduced, strained duck broth and bring to a boil. Reduce heat and simmer. Thicken sauce by whisking the arrowroot dissolved in water into the simmering sauce until the sauce will coat a spoon. Adjust seasoning. About 15 minutes before serving, place boned, halved ducks in a roasting pan with chicken stock to cover the bottom and reheat in a 325-degree oven.

Spoon sauce over the duck halves and serve cooked red cabbage as a side dish.

RED CABBAGE
  6 ounces lean bacon, diced
  6 ounces onion, finely chopped
  4 ounces lard
  6 pounds red cabbage, finely sliced
  3 apples, peeled, cored and sliced
  1 bay leaf
  1 pint red wine
½ cup red wine vinegar
  2 teaspoons sugar
salt to taste
pinch of white pepper

In a large saucepan, sauté bacon and onions in lard until onions are transparent. Add cabbage, apples, bay leaf, wine, ¼ cup vinegar, sugar, salt and pepper then cook together on top of stove for 5 minutes. Cover and braise in a 350-degree oven for 1½ hours. Just before serving, add ¼ cup heated red wine vinegar.

STRAWBERRIES ROMANOFF

SERVINGS: 6
PREPARATION TIME: 20 MINUTES (NOTE ELAPSED TIME)

1 pound fresh strawberries
½ cup Grand Marnier
½ cup cherry brandy
2 pints whipping cream
¼ cup sugar
½ teaspoon vanilla
6 whole fresh strawberries

Wash, stem and dice strawberries. Marinate in Grand Marnier and cherry brandy, covered, for 1 hour. Whip cream until medium peaks form. Add sugar and vanilla and continue to whip to stiff peak stage. Drain the strawberries and reserve the marinating liquid. Fold strawberries into whipped cream. Pour in some of the marinating liquid to give the mixture a creamy texture. Serve in goblets. Garnish with whole strawberries.

CHEF GERHARD BRILL
COMMANDER'S PALACE

*T*he Commander's Palace is a celebration in itself! A huge mansion in the Garden District, it was bought by Ella, Dick, Adelaide, John and Dottie Brennan in 1969 and transformed into one of America's great restaurants.

"When we first saw Commander's we were completely won over by its period charm and fantasy-like Victorian architecture. There were columns, turrets, delicate lacy gingerbread trim, lush gardens and great, spreading trees," says Ella Brennan.

"It was the perfect setting to make Commander's Palace the best restaurant in New Orleans."

There is a calm southern tranquility upon entering Commander's; the gentle courtesy of Dottie greeting guests at the door is inviting and gracious. Downstairs, the three intimate dining rooms were kept practically intact, using original mahogany moldings and Baccarat crystal chandeliers, but shutters were pulled back to let in the light and soft, pale linens were used to

24

cover the walls. Upstairs, the "pow" flavor that Ella uses to describe the unique Creole tastes of food, is apparent in the dining rooms; bright sunshine yellows, crisp apple greens, rosy peach and glossy white were used as wall coverings. A complete wall was replaced with glass to create the Garden Room, overlooking the patio with its flowering shrubs and two-hundred year old oak tree. Creamy lattice work covers the walls and grass green carpeting brings the outdoors inside.

To reach the patio and bar, guests must walk through the kitchen and that is Chef Brill's domain. Born in Stuttgart, Germany in 1939, Gerhard Brill was apprenticed to a great hotel kitchen at the age of 12 before he began the cooking odyssey that took him to Zurich, Rome, Barcelona, Athens, Tehran, Moscow, Peking and Bangkok, the last three as chef at the German embassies. He was brought to the United States in 1965 as executive chef for an Atlanta restaurant and went on to cook for clubs on Hilton Head Island, where he began "cooking southern." That does not mean Creole cooking, which came later when Ella and Dick Brennan invited Gerhard to Commander's Palace as executive chef in 1978.

The message at Commander's is in the menu; the Brennans' and Gerhard constantly develop their Haute Creole cuisine into something unique. The old way of cooking, using heavy roux, gave way to New Haute Creole; the grand classics— gumbos, jambalayas, bisques, and sauces— were refined. Reductions of basic stocks with wines, spices and cream brought out true flavors without sacrificing taste.

Chef Brill absolutely delights in talking about his inventions at Commander's: the Crabmeat cake with oysters in a light Creole sauce and Pernod and a reduction of cream; Oysters Mariniere, lightly simmered in wine and vegetables; and blackened Red fish. But, the old-guard faithful customers with taste buds not yet alive to New Haute Creole will find that the Brennans have not forgotton them. Grilled Wisconsin Duck is boned and served in its velvet sauce of Port and demi-glace along with the famous Dirty Rice; Panéed Veal is breaded and sautéed in favorite New Orleans fashion, served with creamy fettuccine. There is something for everyone.

Saturdays and Sundays are extra-special because Dick Brennan created the Jazz Brunch. Two bands play New Orleans jazz, bright balloons are tied to dining chairs and the menu is the fabulous melange that only the Brennans, Chef Brill and Commander's Palace could produce. The casual elegance is truly southern and the New Haute Creole menu is just as enticing as it could be. ✗

COMMANDER'S PALACE
NEW ORLEANS

MENU

SAUTÉ OF LOUISIANA CRAWFISH
Crawfish tails in a creamy butter sauce

OYSTERS MARINIERE
An elegantly light Commander's oyster specialty

SOFT SHELL CRAB CHORON
Whole deep-fat fried crabs—a New Orleans favorite

POMPANO EN PAPILLOTTE
*Fresh Gulf pompano cooked in a paper bag to retain its natural juices with a cream, shrimp
and oyster sauce presented on the side*

VEAL WITH WILD MUSHROOMS
*Medallions of white veal in a demi-glace with burgundy wine, morels, cepes, chanterelles
and American mushrooms*

PRALINE SOUFFLÉ CRÊPES
Thin dessert crêpes filled with meringue, with a rich pecan custard sauce

Sauté of Louisiana Crawfish

SERVINGS: 4
PREPARATION TIME: 10 MINUTES

CREOLE SEAFOOD SEASONING

2 *tablespoons oregano*
⅓ *cup plus 1 tablespoon salt*
¼ *cup granulated garlic*
¼ *cup black pepper*
⅓ *cup cayenne pepper*
2 *tablespoons thyme*
⅓ *cup plus 1 tablespoon paprika*
3 *tablespoons granulated onion*

Combine all ingredients and mix thoroughly. Reserve. (This recipe makes 2 cups of seasoning and it can be stored indefinitely in the refrigerator if kept in a covered glass jar.)

CRAWFISH SAUTÉ

9 *ounces butter*
1 *pound crawfish, peeled tails*
1 *cup green onions, chopped*
1 *tablespoon Creole seafood seasoning*
1 *tablespoon Worcestershire sauce*

Put all the ingredients into a saucepan and sauté until mixture is creamy and warmed through. Serve immediately.

OYSTERS MARINIERE

24 oysters, shucked
¼ cup oyster water (juice from oysters
    plus water to make ¼ cup)
½ cup shallots, minced
¼ cup parsley, chopped
½ cup white wine
¼ teaspoon black pepper
¼ cup soft butter
 3 tablespoons flour
salt to taste

In a shallow pan, poach the oysters in the oyster water with the shallots, parsley, wine and black pepper. Bring to a boil and cook 1 minute. Blend butter with flour. Stir the butter/flour mixture gently into the oysters until thoroughly blended, about 30 seconds. Adjust seasonings before serving.

SOFT SHELL CRAB CHORON

CREOLE SAUCE
½ cup green pepper, chopped
½ cup red pepper, chopped
 1 cup onion, chopped
 2 cups tomatoes, diced
½ teaspoon tarragon, chopped
½ teaspoon oregano, chopped
½ teaspoon basil, chopped
½ teaspoon thyme, chopped
 2 tablespoons butter
 1 tablespoon Creole seafood seasoning
    (see page 27)
 2 cloves garlic, thinly sliced
 1 teaspoon Tabasco

In a sauté pan, place peppers, onion, tomatoes, tarragon, oregano, basil, thyme and butter. Sauté these ingredients for 1–2 minutes. Before the onion becomes transparent, add the Creole seafood seasoning, garlic and Tabasco. Simmer sauce to reduce the liquid by one-third the volume. Let cool.

BERNAISE SAUCE
 1 cup butter
 4 egg yolks at room temperature
juice of 1 medium lemon
1½ tablespoons Worcestershire sauce
 1 tablespoon white wine
salt and coarse ground pepper to taste

Melt butter in a skillet over medium heat. Do not burn. When completely melted, remove from burner and reserve. Place egg yolks, lemon juice, Worcestershire sauce, wine, salt and black pepper in the top of a double boiler. The water in the bottom pan should just simmer and not touch the top pan. Using a whisk, beat the egg yolk mixture until it thickens and a sheen forms,

(continued)

approximately 3 minutes, but no more than 5 minutes. Remove from heat. In a slow steady stream begin adding the butter, whipping it in with a whisk. Continue until all the butter has been added. The sauce should be light and fluffy. Set aside.

Fold the reduced, cooled Creole sauce into the bernaise sauce. Reserve until serving.

Season crabs with Creole seafood seasoning and minced garlic. Dust with flour. Dip in egg and milk, then into bread crumbs. Using tongs to hold crabs securely, deep-fry in 350-degree oil for about 3 minutes or until golden. Drain on paper towels. Place the crabs on serving plates, spoon the choron sauce over them and serve immediately.

CHORON SAUCE
   1 cup Creole sauce
1¼ cups bernaise sauce

CRABS
   8 large soft shell crabs, cleaned with
      eyes removed
Creole seafood seasoning to taste
   1 clove garlic, minced
   1 cup flour
   1 egg slightly beaten with 1 cup milk
   2 cups bread crumbs
oil for deep-fat frying
2⅔ cups choron sauce

SERVINGS: 4
PREPARATION TIME: 30 MINUTES

POMPANO EN
PAPILLOTTE

PAPILLOTTE SAUCE
   3 ounces butter
   1 clove garlic, minced
   1 tablespoon parsley, chopped
   1 tablespoon green onion, chopped
   1 shallot, minced
  24 oysters
  24 shrimp
   2 tablespoons Creole seafood seasoning
      (see page 27)
   1 tablespoon flour
   4 cups reduced fish stock (or
      combination of clam juice
      and white wine)
   1 cup champagne
   2 cups heavy cream

Place butter, garlic, parsley, green onion, shallot, oysters, shrimp and Creole seafood seasoning in a large sauté pan. Simmer for about 1 minute. Stir in the flour, then add the fish stock, champagne and heavy cream and bring to a boil. Reduce heat to simmer and reduce sauce until it has a smooth consistency, about 10–15 minutes. Reserve.

POMPANO

8 pompano fillets
4 sheets of parchment paper
¼ cup butter
8 medium shrimp
8 raw oysters
*¼ teaspoon Creole seafood seasoning
(see page 27)*

Cut the sheets of parchment paper into the shape of hearts. Butter the inside and place 2 pompano fillets on each heart. Place 2 shrimp and 2 oysters on top of the fillets and sprinkle with Creole seafood seasoning. Fold the paper from the corner in small overlapping folds and place these on an oiled baking pan. Bake in a 350-degree oven for about 15 minutes.

To serve, cut the top of the paper open and fold back. Serve with the papillotte sauce. Sautéed vegetables such as eggplant, broccoli, cauliflower, zucchini and carrots may be served as a side dish.

VEAL WITH WILD MUSHROOMS

SERVINGS: 4
PREPARATION TIME: 20 MINUTES

CREOLE MEAT SEASONING
1½ cups salt
¾ cup granulated garlic
¾ cup black pepper
½ cup cayenne pepper
¼ cup cumin

Combine all ingredients, and mix thoroughly. Reserve. May be stored indefinitely in a glass jar in refrigerator. Makes 3¾ cups.

VEAL AND MUSHROOMS
8 3-ounce veal cutlets, pounded
flour to dredge
3 tablespoons butter
¼ cup shallots, chopped
2 ounces morel mushrooms, sliced
2 ounces cepes mushrooms, sliced
*2 ounces chanterelle mushrooms,
sliced*
*2 ounces Pennsylvania mushrooms,
sliced*
1 ounce brandy
¼ cup red wine
¾ cup demi-glace
salt and pepper to taste

Season veal with the Creole meat seasoning and dredge with flour. Melt butter in a skillet and sauté veal until brown, about 1 minute per side. Add the shallots and mushrooms and sauté another 1 minute. Flame with brandy. Add red wine, demi-glace, salt and pepper. Place veal on warm serving plates. Simmer sauce for another minute, then ladle over veal to serve.

PRALINE SOUFFLÉ
CRÊPES

MERINGUE

1¼ cups egg whites
2 cups confectioners sugar

Whip egg whites with electric mixer until frothy. Gradually add the sugar and beat until stiff peaks form. Set aside.

CUSTARD

½ teaspoon dark corn syrup
1½ teaspoons vanilla
2 eggs
½ cup sugar
1 tablespoon rum
½ teaspoon nutmeg
½ teaspoon cinnamon
2 cups cream
1½ cups pecans, chopped
1 cup meringue

Whisk together corn syrup, vanilla, eggs, sugar, rum, nutmeg, cinnamon and cream to blend well. Stir in the pecans then fold into the meringue. Set aside.

CRÊPES

4 eggs
2 cups flour
½ teaspoon oil, plus some for cooking crêpes
1 tablespoon sugar
2 tablespoons cream
½ cup milk
pinch of salt

Whisk together all the ingredients to form a thin batter. Heat a 7–9 inch skillet or crêpe pan and brush it lightly with oil. Pour a small quantity of batter into the heated pan and then tip the pan so that the batter will spread evenly over the bottom. Cook about 1 minute then turn the crêpe. When the other side is well-browned, slide the crêpe out of the pan onto a plate. Make 16 crêpes and set aside, keeping warm.

ASSEMBLY

Using 8 oven-proof serving plates, place 2 crêpes on each plate and spoon 2 tablespoons custard on each crêpe. Top with ½ cup meringue. Fold crêpe carefully around meringue. Pour additional custard over the crêpes. Place on a rack in a 425-degree oven for 7 minutes or until heated through. Remove and serve immediately.

CHEF GÜNTER PREUSS
VERSAILLES

"*I* run five miles a day; that gets rid of all my anxieties and frustrations," says Günter Preuss, owner and chef of the splendid restaurant, Versailles, in the classic Garden District of New Orleans.

The three dining rooms are elegant, European in style and flavor, loosely patterned after the Palace of Versailles and watched over by Evelyn Preuss. "My wife and I created the restaurant and our lives revolve around it," the chef says, "although no one can cook twenty-four

hours a day. We like to ski in Vail but nothing is left to chance: if anything should go wrong while we are away, I can come in and pick up the pieces."

Günter, it would seem, is the last person whom luck might desert. His training, rigidly European, began at the age of 14. "My father owned a restaurant near Berlin and, after the war, I followed naturally in his footsteps as apprentice in the kitchen of a health spa in West Germany. There was a bed to sleep on and food to eat; no split-shifts or child labor laws, but I stayed and worked and went to school at the same time. My grades were straight "A's" and I still hate to chop parsley!" Young Günter then went to the famed Palace Hotel in St. Moritz. As the hotel business was seasonal, he went on to work in Sweden, France and London, arriving in Kansas City in 1960, sponsored by a local country club.

At this point, the Preuss dream was to make enough money to return to Berlin, but fate, in the form of the Statler-Hilton Hotel, beckoned, and it was off to New York for Günter and Evelyn, he as sous chef, knowing that the move meant going through a whole new apprenticeship. "Hilton gave me my business sense," says Günter, "There were conventions, banquets, room service, breakfasts, lunches and dinners to be served in the dining rooms; it never stopped!" Going from the sauté pan into the fire, Günter accepted the job as executive chef at a big hotel in New Orleans. "We served four-thousand meals a day. I always liked to get out of the kitchen to mingle with the guests to see what they liked and how they liked things done. It was a good lesson and since I was tired of making money for others, it seemed to be the time to open our own restaurant."

The Versailles opened in 1972 with Günter in his kitchen, working with the sensational local products—fresh shrimp, lump crabmeat, salty oysters from the Gulf—creating dishes using his superb knowledge of French cuisine. "We were always developing the menu and listening to our guests; if some didn't like a dish, we would investigate why and then take it off the menu. We didn't and don't take complaints lightly."

The pure luxury of Versailles is evident in all facets of the handsome restaurant.

The bar is formal but cheery, the dining rooms elegant, with their deep ruby-colored walls, crystal chandeliers, lighted wall sconces and heavy draperies. The French dining chairs are covered with satin-striped fabric, the table linen is pristine, the food glorious.

The menu is in French with too brief descriptions of the dishes in English; it would be necessary to taste each offering in order to understand the complex subtleties of the Preuss style.

Günter Preuss is a great chef; his years of training have counted for everything in putting together one of the famous restaurants of New Orleans. The chef says, gently, "It is gratifying to own this restaurant." The true personality comes out in the kitchen, where the chef belongs and where the proof lies in the eating. ✗

VERSAILLES
NEW ORLEANS

CHEF
GÜNTER PREUSS
VERSAILLES

✗

MENU

BOUILLABAISSE
A fish stew with fresh vegetables and saffron

VEAL STEAKS WITH PINK PEPPERCORNS
Braised veal filets in a peppercorn and cream sauce

POACHED PEARS
Whole pears with a raisin and rum filling served with raspberry sauce

✗

Bouillabaisse

SERVINGS: 6
PREPARATION TIME: 45 MINUTES

FISH STOCK
 4 *medium carrots, sliced*
 2 *onions, sliced*
 6 *celery stalks, sliced*
 2 *leeks (white part only), sliced*
 2 *medium green peppers, sliced*
 2 *fennel roots, chopped (if fennel is not available, substitute 2 tablespoons of pernod but add last)*
¼ *cup butter*
 2 *tablespoons tomato paste*
 1 *cup brandy*
 2 *cups white wine*
 3 *tomatoes, peeled, seeded and chopped*
½ *teaspoon garlic, finely chopped*
pinch of saffron (presoaked)
 3 *quarts fish broth*

Sauté carrots, onions, celery, leeks, peppers and fennel in butter until transparent. Add tomato paste. Sauté and flame with brandy. Extinguish flames with white wine. Add tomatoes, garlic and saffron. Add fish broth. Simmer until vegetables are tender, approximately 30 minutes.

(continued)

FISH AND SHELLFISH

1 teaspoon shallots, chopped
1 teaspoon garlic, chopped
1 teaspoon green onion, chopped
1 teaspoon parsley, chopped
2 tablespoons olive oil
1 pound shrimp, peeled
1 pound fish fillets, boneless, skinless
   and cut into 1-inch pieces
6 oysters, shucked
6 medium lobster tails, shelled
   (optional)
20 mussels in shells (optional)
½ cup brandy
2 cups white wine
¼ pound lump crabmeat
salt and pepper to taste
fresh parsley, chopped

Sauté shallots, garlic, green onion, and parsley in olive oil for 1 minute. Add shrimp, fish fillet pieces, oysters, lobster, and mussels and sear for about 1 minute. Flame with heated brandy. Add white wine. Add prepared fish stock and simmer for approximately 10 minutes. Correct seasonings to taste. Top with fresh lump crabmeat and garnish with parsley.

VEAL STEAKS WITH PINK PEPPERCORNS

SERVINGS: 4
PREPARATION TIME: 1 HOUR

VEAL AND SAUCE

4 4-ounce top round or filet veal steaks
juice from ½ lemon
flour to dredge
1–2 tablespoons clarified butter
½ cup white wine
½ cup reduced beef stock
½ teaspoon shallots, chopped
½ teaspoon green onion, chopped
½ teaspoon Dijon mustard
1 teaspoon pink peppercorns
¼ cup heavy cream
salt and white pepper to taste

Pound veal flat. Season with salt and white pepper. Sprinkle with lemon juice and coat with flour. Sauté veal in melted clarified butter (about 2 minutes per side). Drain butter from pan and deglaze with ¼ cup white wine. Remove veal from pan and reserve in a warm place.

To the sauté pan add reduced beef stock, shallots, green onion, mustard and pink peppercorns. Reduce for 1 minute. Put the veal back in the pan. Add cream and adjust seasoning. If the sauce is too thick add more white wine. Reserve.

VEGETABLE GARNISH

1 leek
2–3 baking potatoes
8 cherry tomatoes
½ cup white wine
3 teaspoons butter
1½ teaspoons parsley, chopped
½ teaspoon shallots, chopped
salt and white pepper to taste

HOLLANDAISE SAUCE

3 egg yolks
½ cup white wine
juice of 1 lemon
1 cup butter, clarified and cooled
salt and white pepper to taste

ASSEMBLY

Chop the field cut and green top off the leek. Quarter the white part and simmer in a pan with ¼ cup white wine, 1 teaspoon butter, and salt and pepper to taste for 6–7 minutes.

Peel the potatoes and with a melon ball scoop out 20 small potato balls. Blanch potato balls in boiling salted water to cover for about 5 minutes. They should still be crisp. Drain, then sauté balls in 1 teaspoon butter and chopped parsley for 5–10 minutes.

Sauté whole cherry tomatoes in ¼ cup white wine, chopped shallots, and 1 teaspoon of butter for about 3 minutes. Correct seasoning with salt and pepper. Reserve the vegetables in a warm place.

Mix egg yolks, white wine, lemon juice, salt and pepper in the top of a double boiler over boiling water. Cook and stir until ingredients are foamy and coat a whisk. Slowly add the clarified butter. Adjust seasoning.

In a large casserole dish or on a serving plate arrange the veal steaks and the sautéed vegetables. Spoon the veal sauce over the filets and spoon hollandaise sauce over the leeks. Garnish with fresh parsley.

POACHED PEARS

SERVINGS: 4
PREPARATION TIME: 30 MINUTES

RAISIN FILLING
¼ cup raisins
1 teaspoon sugar
2 tablespoons dark rum

Mix ingredients in a bowl and reserve.

RASPBERRY SAUCE
2 cups whole raspberries
1 cup white wine
juice from 1 lemon
sugar to taste
1 tablespoon cornstarch mixed with
¼ cup water
2 tablespoons cherry brandy

In a saucepan, simmer raspberries, white wine, lemon juice and sugar for 5 minutes. Add cornstarch/water mixture and simmer for another 3–4 minutes. Strain berries and add cherry brandy. Reserve.

PEARS AND POACHING LIQUID
4 ripe pears
1 cup white wine
1 teaspoon sugar
juice and rind from 1 lemon
1 cinnamon stick
½ cup water

ASSEMBLY
4 chocolate cups
1 cup whipped cream
4 cherries

Slice bottoms off pears. Peel pears; remove the cores (through the bottom, leaving the stems intact). Stuff pears with raisin filling. Combine wine, sugar, lemon juice and rind, cinnamon stick, and water in a large saucepan. Add stuffed pears, taking care to stand them upright without losing the raisin filling, and poach for 10 minutes in a 350-degree oven until tender.

To serve, pour a little raspberry sauce into the bottoms of 4 chocolate cups. Top each with a poached pear, steam side up. Spoon remaining raspberry sauce over pears. Decorate with whipped cream and cherries.

CHEF GOFFREDO FRACCARO
LA RIVIERA

Chef Goffredo Fraccaro is that rare combination of actor/clown/perfectionist! His greeting, as he throws up his hands with joy at seeing a favored regular customer or a shy newcomer, is filled with his special sense of welcome. His accent could be cut with a knife. "In 20 years in America I try to speak English but I cannot lose my accent," he says. He shouldn't try, for the lyric quality of his Genoese accent only adds to his charm. Roly-poly, absolutely twinkling with happiness, Goffredo em-

braces almost everyone with the warmth of his personality. He loves his restaurant, his customers, his kitchen, his veal, his lump crabmeat, his two chefs and his staff. Most of all, Chef Fraccaro loves to cook and, for those fortunate enough to find the way to La Riviera in Metairie, the evening unfolds as does an Italian opera.

There is a feeling of controlled high-energy along with the fun, a sense of hard work along with the elegance of the Mediterranean-blue draperies, the creamy wallpaper and huge oil paintings of the Italian Riviera. It is because Goffredo grew up in occupied Italy during World War II. "The main thing was getting through the war," he says somberly, then his eyes light up: "When peace came, I saw the luxury liners in the great port of Genoa, and to go to America, to be a chef, was the great dream of my life. I was young and ambitious and I didn't want to be a dummy." The young Goffredo was on his own and his world became the kitchens of great hotels on the Italian and French Rivieras, the slaughter-house where he learned to carve meat, the bakeries where he learned to make pas-tries, apprenticing without papers or pay-ment.

The young chef went to Miami for a va-cation and on to New Orleans, "I had read about New Orleans, it suggested food to me and when I went there I went wild for New Orleans! I met an Italian family who owned a restaurant in Baton Rouge and, through a little loophole I got my pa-pers and I worked there for eight years." Chef Goffredo met Arthur Wardsworth, whom he hired and trained to become a cook. The two moved, with their families, to New Orleans in 1970 where Goffredo opened a little restaurant across the street from the present La Riviera. "My place had 60 seats and we worked all the time be-cause we served lunch and dinner. I made fresh pastas and my specialty was cala-mari, the Italian favorite; it was crunchy and delicious and if a customer looked ner-vous about eating squid I would tell him to eat the 'Italian onion ring!' "

In 1978, Chef Goffredo built La Riviera. "It was my dream come true. Arthur came with me as chef and I chose the decor; I wanted to invite all my customers to come to my kitchen to talk about the menu, to tell me the food I could create for them." The food reflects his will to learn and his devotion to the taste buds of his customers. God help the person without an appetite at La Riviera; the chef cajoles, pampers, and pleads. His personality is irresistible because he cares about the pal-ates and stomachs of his friends, the cus-tomers.

He says, "People come here from all over America. The first three days in New Orleans they eat French food. Then they come to see me for their 'pasta fix.' Only in America could a foreigner have the oppor-tunity to work, to achieve a dream. I love what I do and the time passes so quickly." And Chef Goffredo dances off to his din-ing room to coax a special little dessert on a friend, to offer a glass of Chianti Classico from his fine cellar to a new customer and to generally make friends with the world. ✗

LA RIVIERA
METAIRIE

MENU

FETTUCCINE ALLA GOFFREDO
Homemade noodles with white cream sauce

SCAMPI
Whole shrimp sautéed in lemon, butter and herb sauce

VEAL PICCATA
Baby veal with lemon butter sauce

CAPONATA ALLA SICILIANA
Sautéd eggplant with onion, olives, capers and celery

RUM CAKE
A layered cake with a cream filling, topped with whipped cream

🤺

SERVINGS: 4
PREPARATION TIME: 30 MINUTES (NOTE ELAPSED TIME)

FETTUCCINE NOODLES
6 cups flour
4 eggs
½ cup water
semolina flour to dust

Put flour into a bowl and make a well. Add eggs and water. Work with hands or wooden spoon until a dough forms and can be made into a ball. Knead for 5–6 minutes, cover with a cloth and let rest for 20–30 minutes. Cut dough in half, and roll one half on a floured board to ⅛-inch thickness. Repeat with other half of the dough. Roll up both halves, chill for 1 hour and cut into ¼-inch wide noodles. Toss noodles with semolina. Cook the noodles in 8 cups boiling salted water for 5 minutes. Drain and reserve.

SAUCE
½ cup butter, melted
½ cup heavy cream
1 cup Parmesan cheese, grated

Heat butter and cream in a pan; do not boil. Add the fettuccine noodles and toss. Add the cheese and mix with a fork and spoon until all the ingredients are well blended and a creamy sauce forms. Serve warm.

SERVINGS: 6–8
PREPARATION TIME: 20 MINUTES

2 pounds large raw shrimp
2–3 tablespoons olive oil
1 tablespoon paprika
3 teaspoons herb sauce (see below)
juice from 1 whole lemon
¼ cup water
½ cup butter
salt and pepper to taste
fresh chopped parsley to garnish

Remove shell from shrimp, except tail. Devein and wash under cold water. Drain on paper towels. Place shrimp in a sauté pan with salt, pepper and olive oil. Toss, sprinkle with paprika and cook covered on top of the stove for about 10 minutes. Drain off oil and add the herb sauce, lemon juice, water and butter to the shrimp. Correct seasonings and serve garnished with chopped parsley and lemon wedges.

(continued)

HERB SAUCE
1 *clove garlic, chopped*
1 *teaspoon oregano, chopped*
1 *teaspoon parsley, chopped*
1 *teaspoon basil, chopped*
1 *teaspoon mint, chopped*
½ *cup olive oil*
2 *tablespoons vinegar*
juice from ½ lemon
salt and pepper to taste

Combine all of the above ingredients. This sauce may be stored, covered, in the refrigerator for up to 1 month.

Veal Piccata

SERVINGS: 6
PREPARATION TIME: 15 MINUTES

12 veal scallops
salt and pepper
flour to dredge
¼ cup olive oil
2 tablespoons beef stock, heated
juice of 1 lemon
3 ounces butter
2 tablespoons parsley, finely chopped

Gently pound the scallops until thin and flat, but not broken. Sprinkle them with salt and pepper. Dredge lightly in flour. Heat olive oil in a wide pan. Add the veal. Turn up the heat and fry the veal quickly. Drain off grease and add the stock, lemon juice, butter and parsley. Stir well and heat the sauce thoroughly. Spoon sauce over veal scallops to serve.

CAPONATA ALLA SICILIANA

¼ cup olive oil
½ stalk celery, chopped
½ medium onion, chopped
½ cup black olives, chopped
½ cup green olives, chopped
 1 large eggplant, diced
¼ cup whole capers
pinch of chopped garlic
 2 large tomatoes, diced
½ cup water
 2 bay leaves
½ teaspoon oregano
salt and pepper to taste

Heat olive oil in a large sauté pan. Add celery, onions, olives and eggplant, then simmer briefly. Add capers, garlic and tomatoes, again simmering briefly. Add water, bay leaves and oregano. Correct seasoning with salt and pepper. Cover and let steam for 3–4 minutes before serving.

RUM CAKE

CAKE
 6 eggs
⅔ cup sugar
1½ teaspoons vanilla
1½ cups flour, sifted twice

Combine eggs, sugar and vanilla in the top of a double boiler. Beat over boiling water for 3–4 minutes. Remove from heat and continue to whip with a mixer on high speed for 8 minutes until mixture becomes thick and doubles in size. Fold in flour. Pour into 3 greased and floured 9-inch round baking pans. Bake for 35–40 minutes at 350 degrees. Cool on a wire rack.

CHERRY-RUM SYRUP

1 cup maraschino cherry syrup (from cherries)
¼ cup rum

PASTILLERA CREAM FILLING

2 cups milk
4 eggs
¾ cup sugar
½ teaspoon grated lemon peel
1 teaspoon vanilla
¼ cup flour

WHIPPED CREAM TOPPING

2 cups whipping cream
2 tablespoons sugar
1 teaspoon vanilla

ASSEMBLY

Chef-Manager Arthur Wardsworth helps Goffredo prepare the Rum Cake

Mix together cherry syrup and rum and reserve.

Scald milk. Combine eggs, sugar, lemon peel, vanilla and flour in a small bowl. Pour in the scalded milk, then transfer this mixture to the top of a double boiler and cook over boiling water, stirring constantly, for 4–5 minutes until mixture becomes thick. Let cool.

Beat whipping cream until stiff peaks form. Fold in sugar and vanilla. Reserve.

Sprinkle each cake layer with cherry-rum syrup. Spread pastillera cream between the layers. Spread whipped cream topping on the top and sides of the cake. Press sliced roasted almonds onto the sides of the cake. Pipe whipped cream onto the top if desired. Refrigerate until serving time.

CHEF CLAUDE AUBERT
LE BEC FIN

Claude Aubert is a chef's chef! His compatriot cooks in New Orleans respect, like and admire Claude and it is no wonder; his manner is courtly, his training impeccable. There is a lovely, classic quality in the menu of Le Bec Fin, his small, very French restaurant across the Causeway from New Orleans.

"I am a French chef," Claude says with great pride.

Born in the south of France near the port of Toulon, Claude was raised on a farm, which he feels contributed to his expertise in selecting the finest products for the restaurants in which he would work as executive chef. As all European-trained chefs must go through rigorous, tough apprenticeships that prepare them for their careers, Claude too, started his training at age 13. "After two years of hard, physical work in my hometown of Vinon, I was sent to the Brittany coast to the kitchen of a great hotel and it literally took six years of intense work until I was made Chef de

Cuisine at the Hotel de la Jette in Toulon."

Until 1963, when Claude began the travels that took him to Africa, he worked as chef in the famous hotel restaurants along the French Riviera. He says, "There was only one style of cooking—classic French. I was trained in that tradition and the "Cuisine Bourgeoise" or sophisticated family-type cooking, using the finest products, was also my specialty."

Claude's fascination with food goes beyond mere development and preparation; his interests lie in the issues of pure taste. "A steak from Charolais has a totally different flavor than one from Texas; the butter in a sauce Bernaise differs when it comes from Lyon or Wisconsin, so I cannot say that I cook completely French." Claude's slight, literal nitpicking goes on to include Nouvelle Cuisine. "We were cooking what they call "Nouvelle Cuisine" thirty years ago, using fresh products always, deglazing always. Of course we used a little flour for the roux; there is nothing wrong with that."

Claude's journeys to Africa took him to Niger, Senegal, Cameroon and Chad. "I was executive chef at four grand hotels for the next eight years; our clientele was not as sophisticated as the French Riviera and the tropical climate forced me to veer away from my classic training and to use exotic local products, but it was very interesting."

In 1971 Claude and his family came to New Orleans "to put down roots," he says. After working as executive chef at both the Louis XVI and Arnaud's restaurants in the French Quarter, Claude bought the small restaurant that he named Le Bec Fin, which means "finicky eater." After he completely renovated the place, building a big stone fireplace in the dining room, Mrs. Aubert decorated the interior in a soft, light country style to complement the french food. "Now I cook my classic

dishes; a bourride of fresh shellfish and pure broth with fennel, tomatoes, potatoes and serve it with aoili and garlic toast, or crisp duckling with a tart orange sauce; I let my customers build their own menu." The menu is classic French with touches of New Orleans; oysters Bec Fin, Shrimp Remoulade, Redfish Bonaparte, Shrimp Creole—Claude's touch with a snap of imagination means the difference between a chef and a mere cook.

And there are always surprises at Le Bec Fin when Claude Aubert has found something fresh in the market. He has taken his thirty years of classic experience in French Cuisine and turned it into a treasure trove in Louisiana. ✗

LE BEC FIN
COVINGTON

MENU

OYSTERS BIENVILLE
Oysters on the half shell with bienville sauce

DUCK À L'ORANGE
Roast duck with orange sauce bigarade

SOUFFLÉ POTATOES
Twice deep-fat fried puffed potatoes

CELERY AND WATERCRESS SALAD WITH ANCHOVY DRESSING
A refreshing green palate cleanser

CRÊPES SOUFFLÉ
Crêpes with fresh strawberries, kiwi and custard cream

✗

BIENVILLE SAUCE
 ¼ cup butter
 ½ cup onion, finely chopped
 1 cup green onion, minced
 1 cup celery, finely chopped
 2 cups fresh mushrooms, chopped
 2 cloves garlic, minced
 2 cups small raw shrimp, peeled
 1 teaspoon thyme, chopped
 1 bay leaf
 1 teaspoon parsley, chopped
few drops Angostura bitters
few drops Tabasco sauce
salt and pepper to taste
 ¼ cup white wine
 1 tablespoon lemon juice
 1 cup heavy cream
roux to thicken (1 cup butter blended
 with 1½ cups flour)
1½ cups bread crumbs

Melt the butter and sauté the onion, green onion, celery and mushrooms until the onion becomes transparent but not brown. Add the garlic and shrimp. Simmer 10 minutes and add the seasonings, white wine, lemon juice and cream. Add the roux a bit at a time until the sauce becomes very thick. Stir in the bread crumbs.

ASSEMBLY
 2 dozen raw oysters, on the half shell
 4 pie pans filled with rock salt

Place 6 raw oysters on the half shell on each of the four pans filled with rock salt. Cover each oyster with Bienville Sauce. If desired, spoon a light glaze of hollandaise or mornay sauce on top. Bake oysters at 400 degrees for about 10 minutes, until the oysters heat through and the sauce starts to brown.

Duck à l'Orange

DUCK Á L'ORANGE

SERVINGS: 4
PREPARATION TIME: 1 HOUR

2 ducklings, about 3 pounds each
1 stalk celery, cut into large pieces
2 carrots, cut into large pieces
1 onion, cut into large pieces
1 whole garlic bulb, halved
½ cup sugar
½ cup red wine vinegar
3 ounces Grand Marnier
3 oranges (peel and julienne the skin of the orange for garnish)
1 ounce arrowroot diluted in ½ cup Chablis wine
2 cups duck stock or demi-glace
8 tablespoons unsalted butter
salt and pepper

Rub salt on the ducklings and set on top of the celery, carrots, onion and garlic in a large roasting pan, breast side up. Put 2 tablespoons soft butter on top of each duckling and roast for 45 minutes at 400 degrees, keeping the meat slightly underdone. Baste every 5–6 minutes. Meanwhile, combine the sugar and red wine vinegar in a saucepan and reduce until the mixture carmelizes. Deglaze with 1 ounce Grand Marnier and the juice of 1 orange. Reduce again and bind the sauce with the arrowroot dissolved in water. Take the roast ducklings out

(continued)

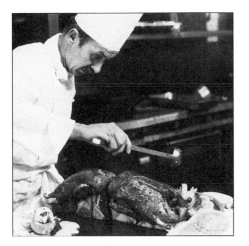

of the pan and keep warm until serving. Drain the fat off the vegetables and deglaze the roasting pan with 2 ounces Grand Marnier. Add the juice from 2 oranges, the duck stock or demi-glace and the carmelized sugar and wine sauce. Boil sauce for a few moments to reduce, then strain into a sauté pan. Reduce again briefly to a nice consistency, whisking in about 4 tablespoons butter. Cover the roast ducklings with the sauce and garnish with julienned orange peel.

SOUFFLÉ POTATOES

SERVINGS: 4–6
PREPARATION TIME: 20 MINUTES

8 large Idaho potatoes
8 quarts frying oil (4 quarts in each of 2 deep kettles or saucepans)

Choose uniform-sized potatoes. Peel and cut potatoes lengthwise into slices ⅛-inch thick. Plunge the slices into the first pan of oil which should be 300–350 degrees. Do not crowd the pan. The slices will sink. Carefully agitate the pan with a shaking motion to keep the potatoes covered with the hot oil. When potatoes rise to the top, remove from oil (process should take about 1½ minutes). Drain slices in a frying basket for 5 minutes or until they reach room temperature. Just before serving, plunge them into the other pan of very hot oil, 425–500 degrees. In a few seconds they will puff up and will turn a golden brown. Drain, spread on a cloth or paper towels to dry. Sprinkle with salt and serve at once.

Note: It may take a couple of batches for the oil to reach the correct temperature to successfully soufflé the potatoes.

CELERY AND WATERCRESS SALAD WITH ANCHOVY DRESSING

2 bunches watercress (cut off the tough
   ends of the stems)
1 celery stalk, julienned
6 mushrooms, julienned
1 carrot, julienned
½ onion, thinly sliced
2 anchovies
1 teaspoon salt
1 teaspoon Dijon mustard
2 cloves garlic, minced
salt and pepper
2 tablespoons red wine vinegar
6–8 tablespoons olive oil
2 tablespoons parsley, minced

Arrange watercress in a bowl with celery, mushrooms, carrot and onion. Mash anchovies to a paste with the salt. Heat a skillet very hot and add the paste. Stir for 30 seconds and put paste in a warm bowl. Add the garlic, mustard, salt, pepper and vinegar. Beat to blend, then add parsley. Drizzle in the oil slowly to form a smooth sauce. Pour over salad.

CRÊPES SOUFFLÉ

CRÊPES
   2 cups flour
2½ cups cold milk
few drops vanilla
½ cup sugar
4 whole eggs
2 egg yolks
pinch salt
melted butter for cooking crêpes

Put the flour and milk into a bowl and stir until smooth. Add the vanilla, sugar, whole eggs, egg yolks and salt. Stir again to obtain a liquid batter. Let rest 30 minutes before cooking. Heat a skillet or crêpe pan, then brush pan lightly with butter and pour in enough batter to cover the bottom with a thin coating. Cook crêpe until brown, about 1 minute. Turn each crêpe and brown the other side, about 30 seconds. Use all the batter and reserve the crêpes in a warm place.

PASTRY CREAM

3 cups milk
1½ cups sugar
1 teaspoon vanilla
6 egg yolks
1 cup flour
pinch salt

Scald 2 cups milk with ½ cup sugar and vanilla. In a bowl, whisk together egg yolks, 1 cup sugar, flour and salt. Add 1 cup cold milk. Add the scalded milk very slowly to the yolk mixture. Transfer to a heavy saucepan and bring to a boil, whisking constantly to prevent scorching. When cream becomes thick, transfer to a bowl and let cool.

SOUFFLÉ FILLING

½ cup strawberries, chopped
½ cup kiwi, chopped
2 ounces Grand Marnier
2 cups pastry cream
8 egg whites
½ cup sugar

Place strawberries and kiwi in a bowl. Pour in the Grand Marnier. Fold in the pastry cream. In another bowl, whip the egg whites to medium peaks. Add the sugar and beat to stiff peaks. Fold the stiff egg whites into the fruit and pastry cream mixture. Reserve.

SABAYON SAUCE

4 egg yolks
⅓ cup sugar
½ cup white wine
1 ounce Grand Marnier

Whisk ingredients together in the top of a double boiler over hot water until creamy and thick. Reserve.

STRAWBERRY SAUCE

½ cup hot water
1 cup strawberry preserves
1½ tablespoons Grand Marnier
1½ tablespoons Crème de Cassis
1 pint strawberries, diced

Combine the water, strawberry preserves, Grand Marnier and Crème de Cassis in a food processor and blend for a few seconds. Pour in a bowl and add strawberries. Reserve.

ASSEMBLY

Place the crêpes on a baking pan. Spoon soufflé filling on each crêpe and fold over. Bake at 275 degrees for 5 to 8 minutes. Spoon sabayon and strawberry sauce over crêpes and serve hot.

THE WONG BROTHERS
TREY YUEN

The five Wong brothers live and work as a team; a strong sense of family is a mirror image of their extraordinary Chinese restaurant, Trey Yuen, in Mandeville, across Lake Pontchartrain. In translation, "the crystal jade green garden," it is literally just that—a beautiful, low, oriental-style house surrounded by waterfalls, pools of clear water filled with darting, golden fish and two huge porcelain dogs guarding the entrance to the restaurant. The doors open to luxurious, beautifully decorated dining rooms in tones of muted apricot, rose and pale gold, separated by railings of carved rosewood and emerald-green foliage.

James, the eldest brother and primary chef, speaks of the family's background:

"We were all born in Hong Kong after my parents escaped from Canton province during the Chinese civil war. My second brother, Frank, and I learned to cook as apprentices in Hong Kong; there was a freedom to create in that city, it was the Paris of the Orient. We all worked, even when we went to school." John, the fourth brother, mused as he said, "I worked as a dishwasher and busboy for twelve years and always wanted to cook, from the times I went grocery shopping with my mother in Hong Kong."

The road to New Orleans was long, winding and difficult. The brothers traveled from Hong Kong to Vancouver to Amarillo to San Francisco—going to school, working, saving money. Finally, in

1971, in Hammond, Louisiana, Frank and John sunk their entire $5,000 savings into a small restaurant they named China Inn. "We had two woks and eleven tables," Frank says, "but we were so self-confident; we wanted to bring our Cantonese feelings of cooking—that seasonings should enhance the flavors of food—to the customers we hoped would come. Our style of cooking was to use the freshest of seafood, fish and vegetables, and to cook dishes that had crisp textures complementing mellow flavors with delicate spices."

Nine years later, in 1980 Frank, John, and James (who had joined the other two brothers) opened the luxurious Trey Yuen. John says, "Our former friends and customers from China Inn came to Trey Yuen bringing their friends," Frank speaks with a smile in his voice. "Now, we don't rest, either. We travel, we eat, we learn more: there are no limits!"

As the serenity of the glowing rosewood and satin textures in the dining rooms of Trey Yuen give the diner those warm feelings of welcome and relaxation, the kitchen is a flurry of flashing cleavers and the sizzle of hot oils. The gas jets under the seven vast woks on the twenty-two foot long gas stove, custom-made in San Francisco, create a high, intense heat of up to 2,000°F. James and John, the chefs, with their sleight-of-hand cooking magic, toss in and turn out the ginger-scented, garlic-spiced dishes they love.

The subtleties of golden brown marinades for each perfectly designed, generours order—whether rosy lobster, tender pork, marbled beef or pearly shrimp, are melded into pure flavors. Gleaming silver holders of jewel-bright vegetables, some star-shaped, some tiny pine tree-shaped, some intricate flower-shapes, wait to be scooped up by the chefs to toss with the meats and fish—carrots, cubes of jade-green peppers, yellow baby corn, crescents of snowpeas, straw mushrooms, hot red chili peppers, crunchy water chestnuts, forest-green slices of crisp zucchini and pale scallions.

Every night, when Trey Yuen closes, when the last customer has said goodbye, the Wong brothers, with their families and their kitchen staff sit down at two huge round tables in one of their beautiful dining rooms, to share food and ideas with each other. They have their rules, responsibilities and that special Chinese sense of family that is, at once, creative and disciplined. Their reputations are solid.

TREY YUEN
MANDEVILLE

MENU

BEEF WITH WATERCRESS SOUP
A light soup made with flank steak and fresh watercress

BARBECUED RIBS
A Cantonese appetizer featuring spareribs and a tangy barbecue sauce

SHRIMP KEW
Shelled shrimp in a wine sauce with an assortment of vegetables

LEMON CHICKEN
Pan-fried golden brown boneless chicken topped with a lemon sauce

LOBSTER IN BLACK BEAN SAUCE
Maine lobster stir-fried Chinese style with an aromatic sauce

✗

Chefs John Wong (left) and Tommy Wong (right)

BEEF WITH
WATERCRESS SOUP

6 ounces flank steak, cut in 1½-inch
   strips
¼ teaspoon salt
1 teaspoon cornstarch
1 teaspoon light soy sauce
1 teaspoon oil
1 teaspoon rice wine or sherry
½ egg white
2 bunches watercress
1 quart chicken broth
1 tablespoon light soy sauce
1 tablespoon oil
salt and pepper to taste

Marinate beef in salt, cornstarch, soy sauce, oil, rice wine or sherry and egg white for 20–30 minutes. Clean watercress thoroughly, and chop off roots. Cut into 1-inch lengths.

In saucepan or wok bring broth to a boil. Add beef and watercress. Bring to a boil again. Add 1 tablespoon soy sauce, 1 tablespoon oil, salt and pepper to taste. Remove from heat and serve.

BARBECUED RIBS

2 racks of spareribs, about 2 pounds
   each
3 tablespoons light soy sauce
1 tablespoon dry sherry
4 tablespoons catsup
1 tablespoon concentrated orange juice,
   undiluted
4 tablespoons sugar
2 tablespoons honey
1 tablespoon hoisin sauce
½ teaspoon five spice powder
2 drops red food coloring

Trim any fat off the ribs and remove the overlapping piece of the meat on the bony side, if any. Lay the ribs flat on a tray and mix the remaining ingredients to form a marinade. Rub the marinade on both sides of the ribs and place in the refrigerator for at least 4 hours, overnight if possible. Place marinated meat on a rack over a pan filled with 1 inch of water to prevent sticking and burning in the oven. Preheat oven to 375 degrees. Roast ribs for 35 minutes. Increase oven to 450 degrees and cook for 10 more minutes. Serve immediately.

SHRIMP AND VEGETABLES

12 ounces medium or large shrimp
1½ teaspoons cornstarch
½ egg white, beaten
1 tablespoon oil
pinch of salt
pinch of white pepper
2 cups oil
3 tablespoons oil
¼–½ teaspoon fresh ginger, minced
½ teaspoon garlic, chopped
½ cup celery, chopped
½ cup straw mushrooms
½ cup baby corn, halved
¼ cup carrots, sliced
½ cup snow peas, strings removed
2 tablespoons rice wine or sherry
gravy mixture (see below)

GRAVY MIXTURE

½ teaspoon salt
½ teaspoon sugar
1 teaspoon oyster sauce
1 tablespoon light soy sauce
½ teaspoon sesame seed oil
1 teaspoon oil
*1½ teaspoons cornstarch dissolved in ½
    cup chicken stock*
dash of white pepper

Peel and devein shrimp. Mix together the cornstarch, egg white, 1 tablespoon oil, salt and white pepper to form a marinade. Toss shrimp in marinade and refrigerate for 30 minutes.

Heat 2 cups oil in a wok, put in the shrimp and toss them rapidly until they are almost cooked. Remove the shrimp from the wok and drain. Drain the remaining oil out of the wok. Reheat the wok and add 3 tablespoons oil. Toss in the ginger and garlic. Put all the vegetables in the wok and stir-fry for 90 seconds. Add the shrimp. Sprinkle with rice wine or sherry and stir for another 30 seconds. Add gravy mixture until sauce thickens. Remove from wok and serve.

Mix together all ingredients and reserve.

3 boneless chicken breast halves
1 teaspoon sherry
1 teaspoon light soy sauce
¼ teaspoon salt
1 tablespoon cornstarch
½ egg, beaten
pinch of white pepper
flour to dredge
½ cup oil
1 tablespoon rice wine
½ teaspoon garlic, minced
1 teaspoon instant custard powder
1 tablespoon sherry
1½ tablespoons sugar
¼ teaspoon salt
1 tablespoon vinegar
½ cup water
½ tablespoon oil
½ teaspoon hot pepper oil
juice and rind of 1 lemon
2 slices fresh ginger, ½-inch in diameter, ⅛-inch thick (optional)
2 teaspoons cornstarch mixed with 2 tablespoons water

Mix together 1 teaspoon sherry, 1 teaspoon soy sauce, ¼ teaspoon salt, 1 tablespoon cornstarch, beaten egg, and pinch white pepper to form a marinade. Marinade chicken pieces in this mixture for 20 minutes. Coat the pieces in flour. Heat wok or heavy skillet and add ½ cup oil. Fry chicken until both sides are golden brown. Add 1 tablespoon rice wine and cover briefly to steam flavors in. Remove chicken from pan and chop into bite-sized pieces. Reheat pan, add garlic and simmer for a few seconds. Combine remaining ingredients (except cornstarch mixed with water) to form a sauce and add to the pan. Add the lemon rind and ginger slices. When mixture comes to a boil, thicken with cornstarch mixed with water. Remove lemon and ginger. To serve, place chicken on plates and cover with sauce.

Chef John Wong

SERVINGS: 4
PREPARATION TIME: 15 MINUTES (NOTE ELAPSED TIME)

6 ounces pork, minced or ground
¼ teaspoon salt
1 teaspoon light soy sauce
½ egg, beaten
1 tablespoon cornstarch
1 tablespoon oil
pinch of white pepper
1½ pound live Maine lobster
1 egg, beaten
3 tablespoons cornstarch
5–6 cups peanut oil
2 tablespoons oil
3 cloves garlic, coarsely chopped
6 slices ginger
6 scallions, cut in 2½-inch lengths, white and green parts separated
1 tablespoon fermented black beans, rinsed and coarsely chopped
2 tablespoons rice wine
¾ cup chicken stock
1 teaspoon light soy sauce
½ teaspoon dark soy sauce
¾ teaspoon sugar
salt and pepper to taste
1 tablespoon cornstarch dissolved in ¾ cup water
½ teaspoon sesame seed oil

Chef James Wong

Marinade pork in ¼ teaspoon salt, 1 teaspoon soy sauce, ½ beaten egg, 1 tablespoon cornstarch, 1 tablespoon oil and a pinch of white pepper for 20 minutes.

Split the lobster in half lengthwise. Remove and discard the stomach sac (a pouch about 1 inch long that is in the head). Keep the greenish tomalley and any roe intact. Apply the whole beaten egg with a brush to both halves of the lobster. Follow with a light coat of cornstarch and set aside.

Heat a wok or heavy skillet over high temperature until hot. Pour in 5–6 cups of peanut oil and heat to 325 degrees. Gently place both halves of the lobster into the wok. Swirl a few times until lobster is 80% cooked. Set lobster aside and drain oil from wok. Reheat wok with 2 tablespoons oil. Add pork and stir vigorously to break up lumps. Keep stirring until meat has lost all pinkness. Toss in garlic, ginger, scallions (white part only) and black beans. Pour in rice wine and add the lobster halves. Pour in the chicken stock and steam-cook until the lobster is completely cooked, about 3–5 minutes. Remove lobster and place both halves on a serving plate. To the wok add 1 teaspoon light soy sauce, ½ teaspoon dark soy sauce, sugar, salt and pepper. Pour the cornstarch dissolved in water into the wok. Add the sesame seed oil and scallions (green parts). Stir in a circular motion until the sauce thickens. Spoon the sauce over the lobster and serve.

Lobster in Black Bean Sauce

CHEF CHRIS KERAGEORGIOU
LA PROVENCE

Chef Chris Kerageorgiou adds a soupçon of laughter, verve and generosity to his delicious French food at La Provençe, along with an understanding of what his diners expect. He gives them comfort and the interior of his restaurant reflects his Mediterranean background. A huge brick fireplace separates the dining room, creating the sense of two cozy rooms. The tables, with snowy cloths, oversized plates from Limoges and good-sized wine glasses are perfect foils for the country crocks of fresh smooth paté and toasty croutons that he serves to each table as a little pre-appetizer. Chris, in his bombastic way,

says, "At my inn we greet you with a smile, seat you with a smile, serve you with a smile and wave goodbye to you with a smile."

One of twelve children of Greek parents living in France, Chris was apprenticed to a baker as a young boy. He hated it. After the war, he enlisted in the merchant marines and jumped ship near San Francisco, with fifty cents in his pocket, no English and no papers. There were certain "street smarts" that young Chris learned and never forgot; the first was not to get caught.

The kitchens of fine hotels in San Francisco seemed a temporary haven and Chris learned the basics of cooking. "I am self-educated," Chris says now, with great pride, and he speaks softly of the years spent washing dishes, and taking odd jobs as a busboy until joining the great ocean liner galleys, always learning, until he worked his way up to Captain in the dining rooms of hotels in New Orleans. "I always said someday I would have a restaurant, my own, to serve the food of southern France to Americans. They would be my customers and I would give back some of what I had been given in this country."

Now he is in his great kitchen, built to his exact specifications. "I never get bored," he says, "I enjoy cooking so much. Everything is fresh in my kitchen. I grow herbs in my garden and I make all the sausages and charcuterie. I always take my cooking colleagues a little present of my homemade sausage when I visit them. I don't like thick sauces so my stocks are very important; they must be pure and full of flavor. I like to read cookbooks, take the classic dishes and make them a little simpler, then teach them to the students who come to my cooking classes."

The menu at La Provençe is classic French with the light touch of the chef apparent in all dishes. The kids, as Chris calls the young men whom he trains, watch him carefully as he creates his own ballet while he works. He is making a new little appetizer because the fresh oysters are so plump. A rich duxelles of mushrooms and wine is heaped on each oyster, warmed in the oven for a moment, then a big spoonful of rich, yellow aioli, fragrant with garlic, tops the duxelles and oyster. The pan is popped under the salamander for a moment, just enough to glaze and then is served—the flavors and textures just as Chris said they would be,

delicious.

There is a camaraderie among the chefs of New Orleans; they call if they need advice or want to give it and they offer to help if one has a problem. Chris says, "People should help each other. What else are we here for?"

There is a spirit of generosity in Chef Chris and his years of working toward his goal of La Provençe are always in his mind. He says, "I come into my kitchen early in the morning and start to think and create and cook. By three o'clock I'm a little pooped so I have a couple of glasses of champagne and take a snooze for a couple of hours with my Doberman, Heidi. She wakes me up at five o'clock and I go back to my kitchen to make the specials for the evening." Chef Chris beams his smile over La Provençe and the world seems a good place. ✗

LA PROVENCE
LACOMBE

MENU

SHRIMP SAUTÉ ST. TROPEZ
A shrimp appetizer in the style of Southern France

QUAIL "ROGER SAVARAN" IN PORT WINE SAUCE
Marinated Louisiana quail in a wine sauce served with baby turnips

SPRING SALAD
A colorful bouquet of fresh julienned vegetables on a bed of assorted lettuces

GÂTEAU SAINT-HONORÉ
An adaptation of a classic French pastry

✗

Shrimp Sauté St. Tropez

SERVINGS: 4
PREPARATION TIME: 30 MINUTES

SHRIMP AND SAUCE
32 *large shrimp*
 2 *tablespoons olive oil*
 2 *shallots, chopped*
 2 *cloves garlic, chopped*
¾ *ounce Ricard (available at liquor
    stores)*
 1 *cup cream*
juice of ½ lemon
½ *tomato, peeled, seeded and diced*

Peel and devein shrimp. Dry thoroughly. In a medium skillet, sauté shrimp in hot oil for about 1 minute. Add chopped shallots and garlic. Deglaze with ½ ounce Ricard. Remove shrimp and add cream and lemon juice to pan. Cook approximately 5 minutes to reduce. Season with salt and pepper to taste. Just before serving, put shrimp back in sauce to reheat them. Remove shrimp and arrange on a serving plate. Add diced tomato and ¼ ounce Ricard to sauce and simmer another minute. Reserve sauce, keeping it warm.

(continued)

VEGETABLE GARNISH

- 1 carrot
- 1 leek (use only the white part)
- 1 red onion
- 1 small zucchini
- 8 string beans
- 2 sprigs fresh fennel
- ¼ cup butter
- 1 teaspoon Ricard

Dice all the vegetables and the fennel and poach lightly in salted boiling water for about 1 minute. Drain water from vegetables and sauté in the butter. Add 1 teaspoon Ricard to flavor.

To serve, spoon the sauce over the arranged shrimp and top with the vegetable garnish. For additional color, decorate the plate with more fresh fennel.

QUAIL 'ROGER SAVARAN' IN PORT WINE SAUCE

SERVINGS: 4

PREPARATION TIME: 30 MINUTES   MARINATE: 2 HOURS

MARINADE, QUAIL, AND SAUCE

- 8 quail (2 per person)
- 2 shallots, chopped
- 4 ounces ruby port
- 4 ounces olive oil
- 2 bay leaves
- 2 sprigs fresh thyme
- 1 sprig fresh rosemary
- 1 ounce olive oil
- ½ cup vinegar
- ½ cup port wine
- ½ cup ruby cabernet (heavy burgundy may be substituted)
- ½ cup cold butter
- salt and coarse black pepper

Clean and debone quail. Place skin side down in a large dish and add shallots, ruby port, 4 ounces olive oil, bay leaves, black pepper, thyme, and rosemary. Cover and let marinate at room temperature for 2 hours.

Heat 1 ounce olive oil in oven-proof pan. Leave marinating ingredients on quail and sear in hot oil on both sides (skin side down first). Season with coarse ground pepper. After quail are browned on both sides place in 400-degree oven and bake for 5 minutes. Do not overcook. Leave quail slightly pink inside. Remove quail from pan and keep warm. Remove fat from pan and deglaze with vinegar. Add port wine and ruby cabernet, then reduce liquid about 5 minutes until it becomes almost a glaze (bubbles will get smaller as sauce reduces). Strain sauce into another saucepan and reduce for 2–3 minutes (being careful not to let all liquid evaporate). Add butter to sauce a bit at a time and whisk until smooth.

TURNIP GARNISH
1 dozen baby turnips
¼ cup butter
½ cup water
1 tablespoon sugar
salt and pepper to taste

Peel bottom halves of the turnips leaving the tops purple. Leave 1½-inch stems on each. Quarter the turnips if they are too large. Wash and pat dry with a towel. Place turnips in a medium saucepan and add butter, water and sugar. Cook covered about 10 minutes until liquid becomes a glaze.

To serve, place quail on a plate, garnish with turnips and spoon sauce over the quail.

SERVINGS: 4
PREPARATION TIME: 15 MINUTES

SPRING SALAD

SALAD
1 head romaine lettuce, quartered
1 head endive, quartered
1 head Boston lettuce, quartered
1 tomato, chopped
1 leek (white part only), julienned
1 yellow zucchini, julienned
1 red onion, julienned
1 zucchini, julienned
1 carrot, julienned
8 broccoli flowerettes
8 cauliflower flowerettes
2 sprigs fresh basil, chopped
2 sprigs fresh parsley, chopped
½ sprig fresh rosemary (leaves only),
  chopped
vinaigrette (see next recipe)
coarse ground pepper

Arrange quarter sections of romaine, endive and Boston lettuce on 4 individual salad plates. Add a quarter chopped tomato to each plate. Refresh all julienned vegetables and chopped herbs in ice water. Drain on towel and add to salad plates. Drizzle vinaigrette on salad and sprinkle with coarse ground pepper.

VINAIGRETTE
1 tablespoon Dijon mustard
¼ cup red wine vinegar
¼ cup lemon juice
1 sprig fresh basil, chopped
1½ cups olive oil
salt and coarse black pepper to taste

Whisk mustard, vinegar, lemon juice, and basil. Slowly pour in olive oil while whisking. Season to taste.

PASTRY DOUGH
2 cups flour
1 cup butter (room temperature)
1 teaspoon salt
2 teaspoons sugar
3 eggs
1 cup water

Blend flour, butter, salt and sugar by hand to a granular consistency. Make a well and add water and eggs. Mix well with the other ingredients. Refrigerate for 1 hour.

CREAM PUFF PASTE
1 cup cold water
½ cup less 1 tablespoon butter
½ teaspoon salt
1 teaspoon sugar
½ cup plus 3 tablespoons flour
16 eggs

Bring water, butter, salt, and sugar to a boil. While mixture is boiling add flour, mixing over low flame for 1–2 minutes. Remove from heat, and add eggs 2 at a time, stirring with wooden spoon until mixture is thick and pulls away from the sides of the pan.

CUSTARD CREAM PASTRY FILLING
4 cups milk
2 whole eggs
3 egg yolks
1 cup plus 2 tablespoons sugar
few drops vanilla
½ cup less 1 tablespoon flour

Place half of the sugar in a 2-quart saucepan. Pour in milk and bring to a boil. Break eggs into a bowl, add egg yolks, remaining sugar and vanilla. Mix until fluffy. Add flour. Pour a little of the boiling milk into the egg mixture to liquify. Combine egg mixture with the rest of the milk and bring to a boil again for a few minutes. Cool in refrigerator.

CARAMEL
2 cups sugar
1 cup water

Bring sugar and water to a boil. Cook over low heat until mixture turns brown and syrupy. When desired stage is reached, cool over ice water to stop cooking process.

WHIPPED CREAM
2 cups whipping cream
½ cup sugar
few drops vanilla

ASSEMBLY
1 pound chopped roasted almonds

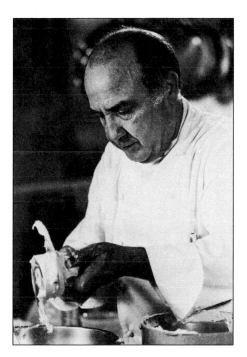

Beat whipping cream until soft peaks form. Add sugar and vanilla and beat until stiff peaks form.

Roll out the pastry dough to form a 9-inch circle. Put this on a buttered and floured baking sheet. Prick holes in the pastry dough with a fork. Put the cream puff paste into a pastry bag and pipe a ring on top of the pastry dough along the outside edge. Form two more concentric rings inside about 2 inches apart. Butter another baking sheet and pipe the remaining cream puff paste onto this forming small cream puffs about 1-inch in diameter. With a fork dipped in water, flatten the cream puffs and the circles of cream puff paste. Bake both sheets of pastry for 20–25 minutes in a 400-degree oven. With a small knife poke holes in the bottom of the baked cream puffs. Fill the holes with the custard cream pastry filling. Dip the bottoms of the cream puffs in caramel and then into chopped roasted almonds (you will need about 1 pound). Fill the center of the baked ring of pastry dough with custard cream pastry filling. Arrange the cream puffs around the edge of the pastry dough (on top of the ring of cream puff paste). Fill in the center of the ring to the top of the cream puffs with whipped cream. Garnish with chopped cherries.

CHEF ROLAND HUET
CHRISTIAN'S

*R*oland Huet has the charm and the accent of movie great Charles Boyer, but his acting takes place in the kitchen of Christian's Restaurant. His subtleties of performance are evident to each diner, the involvement with his menu and each dish to be served are as vital to him as a difficult part is to an actor.

While Roland the chef is happy translating the seductively simple-sounding dishes into glorious, subtle food, Christian Ansel, the owner, talks about his own background. He was an engineer living and working in Paris and he returned to New Orleans in 1969 to be manager of Galatoire's, his family restaurant. In 1973 Christian opened his first restaurant, where he could create and serve what he wanted without being bound by the traditions of Galatoire's. Christian's was successful, but a desire to move to the Mid City district of New Orleans prompted

Chris to buy an old church from a congregation and turn it into the second Christian's. Chris says, "We retained the architectural features of the church, painting the exterior a soft peach and we used European church colors inside to accentuate the structure." It is a charming setting for Chef Roland's fine food.

The chef was born in Blois in France's Loire Valley and sums up his career by saying, "I went into the kitchen when I was six years old and it was like falling in love for the first time." The dream of young Roland was to go to Paris and, after apprenticing in restaurant kitchens, he finally went to work at three-star restaurants, Drouant and Lucas Carton. After thirty years of celebrated cooking in France, Roland Huet met Chris Ansel and the two are now happily ensconced at Christian's.

Roland has adapted his training to the special tastes of New Orleans Creole food and the marriage of both cuisines has found a home on the menu. Chris says, "Ninety per cent of our customers order seafood and we cold-smoke our own redfish and salmon." This innovative manner of generating the smoke of hickory chips and keeping the temperature below eighty degrees insures a delicious texture and gives a light smoky flavor to the fish.

"I love cooking, I love to work on the line every night," says Roland. "I know the people who come to Christian's and I like to make them little surprises; maybe a fillet of trout stuffed with crabmeat and shrimp, served with a light garlic-mayonnaise sauce or a fillet of redfish with a julienne of mushrooms and artichokes in hot, brown butter."

There are more wonderful surprises: the horseradish sauce for his cold, poached redfish has chopped pecans added to the sour cream mixture for crunch and his Chicken in Blackberry Vinegar has a fresh, piquant flavor. Bouillabaisse is filled with local redfish, trout, shrimp, oysters and crabmeat flavored with leeks and garlic. "It has a New Orleans taste, but I serve it the French way with croutons and a classic rouille," Roland says.

Roland Huet and Chris Ansel seem to have the recipe for success. Along with energy, devotion, dedication and a sense of authority, the chef simply says, "People should cook in a classic way with a little twist; I do that and I please the customers and myself." Roland neglects to mention his forty-five years of experience in the kitchen! ✗

CHRISTIAN'S
NEW ORLEANS

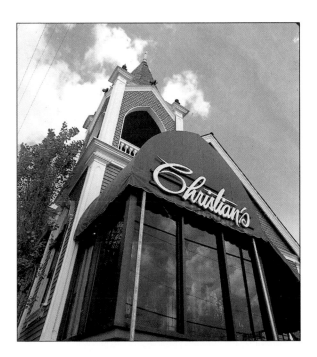

MENU

OYSTERS ROLAND
Oysters served with warm mushroom and garlic butter

OYSTER CHOWDER
A creamy oyster and potato soup

SMOKED REDFISH
Poached smoked redfish in a wine butter sauce

FRENCH-FRIED EGGPLANT
A quick vegetable side dish made with fresh eggplant

BAKED ALASKA
A classic ice cream dessert topped with meringue

✗

SERVINGS: 10
PREPARATION TIME: 30 MINUTES

MUSHROOM/BUTTER MIXTURE
¾ *pound fresh mushrooms (or a 12-ounce can mushroom pieces with juice)*
2 *cloves garlic*
1 *bunch parsley*
2 *cups butter, softened*
1 *cup breadcrumbs*
¼ *teaspoon nutmeg*
1 *teaspoon salt*
1 *teaspoon black pepper*

Pulse mushrooms, garlic and parsley in food processor until finely chopped. Add butter, pulse again until blended well. Add breadcrumbs, nutmeg, salt and pepper. Reserve.

OYSTERS
5 *dozen blanched oysters*

Cook oysters in their own juices until just simmering, about 5 minutes (edges will curl when they are done). Cool in the juices to prevent drying, then drain on a cloth.

Place 6 oysters each in 10 4½-inch au gratin dishes. Smooth mushroom/butter mixture over oysters and place under broiler until brown and bubbly. Serve immediately.

SERVINGS: 4
PREPARATION TIME: 45 MINUTES

½ *green pepper, chopped*
1 *stalk celery, chopped*
½ *yellow onion, chopped*
½ *cup butter*
1 *level teaspoon garlic, chopped*
2 *tablespoons flour*
1 *bay leaf*
¼ *teaspoon thyme*
1 *cup white wine*
2 *cups oyster-water (juice from oysters with enough water to make 2 cups)*
2 *cups oysters*
2 *medium potatoes, diced*
2 *cups whipping cream*
1 *tablespoon parsley*
salt and pepper to taste

Sauté green pepper, celery and onion in butter until transparent. Add garlic, flour, bay leaf and thyme and let simmer briefly. Add wine and oyster-water. Cook until vegetables are tender, about 15 minutes. Meanwhile, in another pan, blanch oysters in their own juices just until their edges curl. Do not overcook. Dice and set aside. Strain oyster juice through cheesecloth and reserve. Boil diced potatoes separately in salted water until tender. Add the poached diced oysters and the potatoes to the vegetables in oyster water. Add the oyster juice, cream,

(continued)

Smoked Redfish

and parsley and simmer until re-
heated thoroughly. Do not boil.
Correct seasonings and serve.

SMOKED REDFISH

SERVINGS: 4
PREPARATION TIME: 20 MINUTES (NOTE ELAPSED TIME)

SMOKING INSTRUCTIONS
4 6-ounce redfish fillets, skinned
2 cups water
1 tablespoon salt

Soak the fillets in the water and salt
for 1 hour. Meanwhile, start a small
charcoal fire in a smoker and soak
some hickory chips in water for at
least 15 minutes. When the coals
are ready, spread the hickory chips
evenly over the coals. Put a pan of
ice in the smoker to insure the temperature in the smoker does not go
above 90 degrees during the smoking of the fish. Put the fillets on a

(continued)

rack and smoke for 40 minutes to 1 hour. Check temperature frequently. If it rises above 90 degrees, open hood to cool. Keep smoked fish refrigerated until ready to poach.

POACHING AND SAUCE
the 4 smoked redfish fillets
1–1½ cups white wine
12 shrimp, peeled and cooked
12 fresh oysters
½ cup butter
1 tablespoon parsley

In an oven-proof sauté pan, poach the redfish fillets in white wine almost to cover in a 375-degree oven until the fillets flake, about 3–4 minutes per side. Remove redfish from pan and keep warm until serving. On top of the stove, bring liquid remaining in sauté pan to a boil and add shrimp and oysters. Thicken liquid with butter. Add chopped parsley and correct seasoning. To serve, spoon sauce and seafood over fillets.

SERVINGS: 4
PREPARATION TIME: 30 MINUTES

FRENCH-FRIED
EGGPLANT

1 large eggplant
flour to dredge
4 egg whites
1½ cups milk
2 cups bread crumbs
2–3 cups peanut oil
salt and pepper to taste

Peel and cut the eggplant into long ½-inch strips. Dredge the strips in flour. Combine the egg whites and milk to make an egg wash. Dip the eggplant strips in the egg wash, then in the bread crumbs. Make sure the strips are covered completely with breading. Fill a deep pot with the peanut oil. Heat to 375 degrees. Cook the strips, turning them frequently, until golden brown (about 7–8 minutes).

Seasoned with salt and pepper; can be served as a vegetable. Seasoned with powdered sugar, this can be served as an hors d'oeuvre.

Baked Alaska

Servings: 12
Preparation Time: 1½ hours (note elapsed time)

GENOISE CAKE

12 eggs
1½ cups sugar
1¼ cups flour (10 ounces)

Beat together eggs and sugar in the top of a double boiler over simmering water until fluffy and smooth. Take it off the heat and mix until full volume is reached and the mixture is cool. Fold in the flour one third at a time. Place in a buttered and floured 9 × 12-inch cake pan and bake at 350 degrees for about 35 minutes. Cake is done when it has puffed, turns golden brown and shrinks away from the sides of the pan. Cool cake on a rack and then freeze it for at least 2 hours, overnight if possible.

RUM SYRUP

1 cup water
½ cup sugar
2 tablespoons dark rum

Combine the above ingredients and reserve.

MERINGUE
  1 cup egg whites
  ¼ teaspoon cream of tartar
  2 cups sugar

ASSEMBLY
1½ quarts ice cream

Place egg whites and cream of tartar in a mixer and beat until stiff. Add sugar and whip on high speed until meringue forms stiff peaks. Reserve.

Slice the frozen genoise cake in half vertically then slice the halves horizontally to make 2 or 3 layers. Brush rum syrup over each cake layer. On a 16-inch oven-proof plate, place the bottom layer of the cake. Top with a layer of ice cream, then another layer of cake. Continue alternating ice cream and cake layers ending with a final layer of cake on top. (Chocolate sauce may also be used as a layer.) Be sure to work fast so the ice cream does not melt. Place in the freezer at least 1 hour. Cover completely the top and sides of the cake with meringue. Just before serving, brown the meringue in a 500-degree oven being careful not to burn it. Slice and place on cold plates to serve.

CHEF GERARD THABUIS
LA SAVOIE

Downhill racer, chef to President de Gaulle, restauranteur Gerard Thabuis of La Savoie in Metairie, has excelled. With typical joie de vivre, he talks about his life in jet-fast sentences.

"I was born in Annecy in 1947 and was a member of the French ski team at age 14, when I had a very bad accident at Innsbruck in 1963," Gerard says. "After that, I signed on as apprentice in the kitchen of the three-star restaurant Le Père Bis in Talloire. I was a gofer, taking orders from the chef and doing the things no one else wanted to do. I made seven dollars a month but the chef and staff saw how I worked and began taking me out to bars with them. It was fun and I was young, so when a saucier or sauté cook left, I was moved into their spots."

Gerard, sitting in his new restaurant relaxing with a glass of champagne, talks of his days as personal chef to President de

Gaulle. "He liked very simple food, roasts of veal, boiled fish and vegetables," Gerard says.

After a stint in the army Gerard went directly to La Table du Roy in Paris, as executive chef. Gerard and the entire kitchen staff were then hired by Aristotle Onassis, a regular customer at the restaurant, to cook at his new hotel on a small Greek Island for one month. These adventures meant seeing the world for the young chef.

Gerard continues his tale: "I had met Linda, my wife, while working for de Gaulle. She lived in Houston and I dreamed of coming to the United States. I loved to travel, I had been all over Europe, and I set my own goal to go to America because I believed that a person could do anything he set out to do." His luck in America began with his marriage to Linda, the appointment as executive chef at Brennan's in Houston in 1971, and four years later at the world-known Brennan's in New Orleans. Roots were put down and his daughter, Nathalie, was born in 1977.

A seemingly inevitable telephone call from Warner Le Roy, entrepreneur/owner of Maxwell's Plum in New York, arrived and Gerard recalls it with great gusto. "Warner called me at six in the morning; he said he needed me as chef at his new restaurant in New York. He had a first-class ticket waiting for me at the New Orleans airport and a big limousine waiting in New York. How could I refuse?" Gerard says that his year at Tavern-on-the Green was the greatest experience of his life. Going to Broussard's in New Orleans for the next five years gave Gerard more experience, and the time to look for the perfect place to open La Savoie.

"I like to walk around my restaurant and talk to my customers," say Gerard. "I like to make special things for them, to change a sauce, to custom-tailor a dish for them. I cooked too french when I first opened, my food was too rich. Now I have learned to adapt to the tastes of my customers, french with the products of New Orleans."

Gerard, when he isn't cooking lunch and dinner at La Savoie, somehow finds the time to ski, fly jets, own a seafood company and two hotels in France. The young chef loves to experiment with food and with life. He says about La Savoie, "I give a piece of my heart when I create a dish and I like to think I have made a friend when a customer loves my cooking." ✗

LA SAVOIE
METAIRIE

MENU

COLD CANTALOUPE SOUP
A refreshing summer soup featuring puréed melon

MARINATED SALMON DANISH STYLE
Salmon marinated slowly in beer with asparagus mayonnaise

OYSTERS LA SAVOIE
Oysters in a pastry shell with saffron sauce

STUFFED FLOUNDER
Whole flounder stuffed with crabmeat and crawfish dressing

MARQUISE AU CHOCOLAT
Molded chocolate spongecake filled with chocolate cream

✗

COLD CANTALOUPE SOUP

SERVINGS: 4
PREPARATION TIME: 10 MINUTES

1 cantaloupe, chilled
2 ounces lemon juice, chilled
1 cup orange juice, chilled
juice of 1 lime, chilled
salt and pepper to taste

Slice cantaloupe in half, remove seeds and rind. Dice pulp and purée in food processor. Add remaining ingredients and blend until smooth. Chill and pour into bowls garnished with mint leaves and slices of lime.

Marinated Salmon Danish Style

SERVINGS: 8
PREPARATION TIME: 25 MINUTES (NOTE ELAPSED TIME)

ASPARAGUS MAYONNAISE
3 egg yolks
⅓ bunch asparagus, cooked and
    rough chopped
3 ounces lemon juice
1 cup olive oil
salt and pepper to taste

In a food processor, blend the yolks, asparagus and lemon juice. Still blending, add the olive oil and mix well. Season with salt and pepper. Makes about 2 cups.

SALMON
1 5-pound salmon, filleted
2 ounces saltpeter
1 cup sugar
½ cup salt
½ cup black pepper
2 tablespoons basil, chopped
2 12-ounce cans beer
asparagus mayonnaise

Place fish skin side down in a flat container. Sprinkle on saltpeter, sugar, salt, black pepper and basil. Pour beer over to cover. Cover the dish and marinate the salmon for 2 weeks in the refrigerator. Drain. To serve, slice salmon very thin, place on a bed of lettuce and spoon on asparagus mayonnaise. Garnish with tomato and lemon slices if desired.

83

OYSTERS LA SAVOIE

1 sheet puff pastry, approximately
   10 × 15 inches
¼ cup butter, melted
2 dozen oysters with oyster water
3 ounces mushrooms, diced
pinch of saffron
pinch of curry powder
3 ounces heavy cream
1 ounce cornstarch
salt and pepper to taste

Cut the sheet of puff pastry into 8 rectangles, roughly 3 × 5 inches. Cover a baking sheet with buttered parchment paper and place 4 of the pastry rectangles on it. Brush pastry with melted butter and top each rectangle with another rectangle of pastry. Press the two halves together gently and bake for 10–15 minutes in a 350 degree oven.

Bring oysters, oyster water, mushrooms, saffron and curry powder to a boil. Boil for 5 minutes, add half of the cream and bring mixture back to a boil. Mix the remaining cream with the cornstarch and stir it into the oysters. Bring to a boil again, stirring. Reduce heat and keep warm until serving. To serve, split the baked puff pastry rectangles in half horizontally and spoon the oysters into the bottom half of the pastry shell. Cover the oysters with the top of the pastry shell and spoon sauce around the bottom of the plate.

4 small flounders, about 12–16
ounces each
4 tablespoons celery, chopped
4 tablespoons parsley, chopped
6 tablespoons green onion, diced
2 bay leaves
¼ teaspoon basil
¼ teaspoon thyme
8 mushrooms, sliced
2 bread rolls, about 4 inches long
each, chopped
1 cup half and half
2 eggs
1 tablespoon garlic, minced
1 cup white wine
12 ounces crab meat
12 ounces crawfish tails, peeled
2 ounces Parmesan cheese, grated
1½ cups butter, softened
½ cup plus 2 tablespoons lemon juice
4 tablespoons Madeira sauce (brown
gravy may be substituted)

Chop the head, tail and fins off the
fish. Make an incision down the
middle of the dark side of the fish
and with a knife separate fish from
bone only to the fin. Lift open and
remove bones. Set aside. Place
celery, parsley, green onion, bay
leaves, basil, thyme, sliced mushrooms, chopped bread rolls, half
and half and eggs into a food processor and blend. Add garlic and ½
cup wine and blend again briefly
to mix. Put mixture in a bowl and
add crabmeat, crawfish tails and
Parmesan cheese. Put mixture into a
baking dish and spread ¼ cup butter on top. Bake for 30 minutes at
450 degrees.

Stuff flounders with baked dressing and put in an oven-proof pan,
then add ½ cup white wine, ¼ cup
butter and ¼ cup lemon juice. Bake
flounders for 10 minutes in a 450-
degree oven.

When baked, remove skin and
any remaining bones. Keep warm
until serving. In a saucepan whisk
together ¼ cup plus 2 tablespoons
lemon juice and the Madeira sauce.
Gradually whisk in 1 cup of butter
and keep hot but do not allow to
boil. To serve, place stuffed flounders on plates and spoon sauce
around each fish.

CHOCOLATE SPONGECAKE
10 *whole eggs*
10 *egg yolks*
 1 *cup oil*
¾ *cup plus 2 tablespoons sugar*
 1 *cup plus 3 tablespoons flour*
½ *cup cocoa*
¼ *cup cornstarch*
½ *teaspoon baking soda*

Sift dry ingredients together. Whip whole eggs, egg yolks, oil and sugar in the top of a double boiler over low heat with a mixer at high speed until mixture is pale yellow and forms a ribbon. Remove from heat and slowly add dry ingredients. Pour batter into a well-buttered 10 × 15 inch cake pan and bake for 40 minutes at 325 degrees. Remove from oven and cool in pan for 5 minutes. Remove cake from pan and allow to cool thoroughly on rack.

CHOCOLATE CREAM FILLING
 5 *ounces semisweet baking chocolate*
 6 *tablespoons strong black coffee*
 7 *egg yolks*
 1 *cup sugar*
1¼ *cups butter, melted*
 ¾ *cup cocoa*
 2 *cups heavy whipping cream*
 ¼ *cup powdered sugar*

Stir the semisweet chocolate and coffee in a saucepan set over almost simmering water until chocolate is melted and smooth. Mix yolks and sugar together in a bowl, whipping until mixture becomes a glossy, pale yellow. Cool the chocolate and coffee and mix into the egg yolk mixture. In another bowl, mix the melted butter and cocoa then fold into the chocolate and egg yolk mixture. Whip the cream to soft peaks. Add the powdered sugar and whip to stiff peaks. Fold whipped cream carefully into the chocolate mixture. Reserve.

GRAND MARNIER SAUCE
1 cup heavy whipping cream
1 cup sugar
grated rind from 1 orange
1 cup orange juice
½ cup Grand Marnier
few drops yellow food coloring

Combine all the ingredients in a bowl and mix well. Reserve.

ASSEMBLY
4 cups strong black coffee
Grand Marnier sauce

Slice spongecake into ½-inch thick strips and brush with the coffee. Line the bottom and sides of a 5 × 9 inch loaf pan with waxed paper cut to fit. Cover the bottom and sides of the pan with the strips of cake. Spoon the chocolate cream filling over the cake strips. Cover the top with more coffee-soaked cake strips. Cover with aluminum foil and place a 1-pound weight on the top. Refrigerate overnight. Remove the aluminum foil and reverse dessert on a serving platter to unmold. To serve, pour the Grand Marnier sauce on the bottom of the serving plates and place the sliced marquise on top.

CHEF MICHAEL ROUSSEL
BRENNAN'S

"*B*reakfast at Brennan's is a daily love affair with our customers and we serve dinner, too," beams Chef Michael Roussel, as he talks of his twenty-eight year "apprenticeship" with the Brennan family.

Brennan's, in its years in the French Quarter, is famed as much for family and friends as for food and service. After the last breakfast was served at the old Brennan's on Bourbon Street in 1956, a swinging jazz band led a procession carrying chairs, silverware, linens and dishes to the new restaurant on Royal Street, to the beat of "When the Saints Go Marching In." Lunch commenced, with favorite patrons drifting in the door toward the bar at noon for their eye-openers of Absinthe Suissesse and Sazarac cocktails.

The larger-than-life legend of the Brennans' southern hospitality is alive today and Michael is the warm custodian of the big kitchen. He was born in New Orleans, and his fond recollections of his family's lunches sparked a fascination with food and its preparation. "In the old days," he says, "Sunday was the only day we all sat down together. The big table was filled with platters of grillades and grits, roasted and stewed chickens, potatoes and yams, biscuits and greens, and lemon and apple pies. We ate simple, country food but it was delicious." Married to Miss Josephine Jalibare in 1961, Michael was drafted into the army and was assigned to work with the former chef at The Antler's Hotel in Colorado Springs. He went to the Cook and Bakers School at Fort Lee, Virginia, graduating with honors and was promoted to Head of Mess at Fort Carson in Colorado.

After an honorable discharge from the army, Michael, the former Assistant Head Waiter at Brennan's, returned as First Apprentice to Chef Paul Blange, the famed chef who had created the original, distinctive menu with Owen Brennan Senior. Over the next eight years, having worked and learned from Chef Paul, Michael accepted the invitation of Ella, Dick, John and Dottie Brennan to become Chef at Commander's Palace. He stayed for five years, then his homing-pigeon instincts took him back to Brennan's and its owners, Owen Junior, Theodore and James.

Since Brennan's can serve one thousand breakfasts and four-hundred dinners in one day, the operating logistics of orders, kitchen preparation and serving could be a nightmare. Consider only one guest ordering: Oysters Casino, each oyster opened, a tangy sauce spooned over and baked; best-seller Tournedos Chanteclair, three prime filets, cooked to order, each served with its distinctive sauce; the Berny potato, a Brennan-inspired crisp, golden ball of mashed potato flavored with chopped green onion and ham, then rolled in ground almonds and deep-fried; assorted vegetables; and, lastly, Bananas Foster, a flaming dessert of bananas, rum, butter, banana liqueur and brown sugar.

"We have a unique team," Michael says, "The Maitre d's, captains, waiters and the cooks function as a well-oiled clock. Each guest who walks through the front door is treated as an honored friend. It is the tradition of the Brennan family that people feel at home in the restaurant."

Chef Michael Roussel is securely in control of his kitchen and he blithely goes off to supervise the making of sixteen gallons of Hollandaise sauce, to be served at an average Sunday breakfast at Brennan's. ✗

BRENNAN'S
NEW ORLEANS

MENU

ABSINTHE SUISSESSE
A traditional New Orleans eye-opener

OYSTER SOUP
A Brennan's specialty featuring Louisiana oysters

EGGS HUSSARDE
Poached eggs atop Holland rusks, Canadian bacon and marchand de vin sauce, topped with hollandaise sauce

EGGS ST. CHARLES
Poached eggs on crisply fried trout with hollandaise sauce

EGGS SARDOU
Poached eggs atop creamed spinach and artichoke bottoms with hollandaise sauce

GRILLADES AND GRITS
Sautéed beef or veal in a spicy Creole sauce served with grits

BANANAS FOSTER
Sautéed bananas flamed in rum and banana liqueur served over ice cream

✗

SERVINGS: 3–4
PREPARATION TIME: 3 minutes

½ cup Herbsaint, Pernod or Ricard
   liqueur
1 large egg white
¼ cup half and half
¼ cup simple syrup (see next recipe)
1 cup crushed ice

Put all the ingredients into a blender and mix on high speed for 30 seconds. Serve in old-fashioned or wine glasses.

SIMPLE SYRUP
¼ cup sugar
1 cup hot water

Combine the sugar and water. Mix until sugar melts. (This syrup can be stored, covered, indefinitely.)

SERVINGS: 8
PREPARATION TIME: 45 minutes

1 cup butter
2 tablespoons garlic, finely chopped
2 cups celery, finely chopped
1 cup green onions, finely chopped
4 bay leaves
1¼ cups flour
12 cups oyster water (the oyster liquor plus sufficient water to make up 12 cups)
4 dozen large oysters, freshly shucked
2 teaspoons salt
1 teaspoon white pepper
2 tablespoons parsley, chopped

Melt the butter over medium heat in a 6-quart heavy saucepan. Sauté the garlic, celery and green onions until tender but not browned, stirring frequently. Add the bay leaves and gradually stir in the flour. Cook 3 minutes longer, stirring constantly, over low heat. Add the remaining ingredients and simmer for 20 minutes. Remove from heat and scoop out the bay leaves with a slotted spoon and discard. Serve immediately.

MARCHAND DE VIN SAUCE
1¼ cups butter, melted
  1 tablespoon garlic, finely chopped
  1 cup white onion, finely chopped
  1 cup boiled ham, finely chopped
  1 cup mushrooms, finely chopped
  1 cup green onion, finely chopped
  3 bay leaves
 ½ teaspoon black pepper
  1 teaspoon salt
  1 tablespoon paprika
  1 tablespoon thyme
  2 tablespoons tomato paste
1½ cups flour
 ¼ cup Worcestershire sauce
  1 quart beef stock
  1 cup dry red wine
1¼ cups parsley, finely chopped

HOLLANDAISE SAUCE
  8 large egg yolks
  4 tablespoons lemon juice
  1 teaspoon salt
about ¼ teaspoon cayenne pepper
1½ pounds butter, clarified
pepper to taste

POACHED EGGS
16 large eggs
 3 quarts water
 2 cups white vinegar

Melt the butter in a heavy saucepan over low heat. Add the garlic and onions and cook until the onions are slightly soft. Add the ham, mushrooms and green onions and sauté for about 2 minutes. Stir in the bay leaves, black pepper, salt, paprika, thyme and tomato paste. Sprinkle in the flour and cook for about 4 minutes. Add the Worcestershire sauce, beef stock, red wine and parsley. Mix thoroughly and simmer over low heat, stirring frequently, until the sauce is very thick and a rich brown color, about 1 hour. Keep warm until serving.

Place the egg yolks, lemon juice, salt and cayenne pepper in the top of a double boiler over simmering water. Beat the mixture with a whisk until the eggs begin to thicken. Remove the double boiler from the heat and slowly add the hot melted butter, beating constantly until the sauce reaches a thick consistency. Adjust seasonings and keep warm over hot water until serving.

To poach the eggs, bring the water and vinegar to a boil in a large skillet or sauté pan. Keep the water at a continuous low rolling boil, crack the eggs into the water. Cook until the egg whites are firm, about 2 minutes. Lift the poached eggs out of the water with a slotted spoon, allowing the water to drain back into the pan. Place them on a triple thickness of paper towels while you assemble the dishes.

ASSEMBLY

8 slices of grilled Canadian bacon or ham
8 slices of grilled tomato
8 slices Holland rusks or toast

To assemble the dish, first place a slice of toast on each warmed plate, then top with a slice of grilled ham or bacon. Ladle about ⅓ cup marchand de vin sauce over meat. Carefully place 2 poached eggs side by side on the sauce, then top with about ½ cup hollandaise sauce. Garnish with grilled tomato slices and serve.

EGGS ST. CHARLES

SERVINGS: 8
PREPARATION TIME: 25 MINUTES

4 trout fillets, (any white-fleshed fish will substitute)
1¼ cups milk
1½ cups flour
1 teaspoon salt
¼ teaspoon black pepper
vegetable oil
16 poached eggs (see page 92)
hollandaise sauce (see page 92)

Soak the fillets in milk for about 5 minutes, then roll in the flour, salt and pepper to coat evenly. Sauté in hot oil (375 degrees) until crisp and nicely browned, about 5 minutes. Remove from the oil with tongs or a skimmer, allowing the excess oil to drain off. Place the fillets on paper towels to drain. To serve, place a piece of trout on each plate, top with 2 poached eggs, then cover evenly with hollandaise sauce.

EGGS SARDOU

SERVINGS: 8
PREPARATION TIME: 30 MINUTES

CREAMED SPINACH

1 cup butter
1½ cups white onions, chopped
8 cups cooked, drained spinach, chopped
1¼ cups flour
4 cups milk
about 1 teaspoon salt
about ½ teaspoon black pepper
½ teaspoon nutmeg

Melt the butter over low heat in a heavy saucepan. Add the chopped onion and cook just until soft. Stir in the chopped spinach and simmer until hot, about 10 minutes.

Add the flour gradually, stirring constantly. Add the milk, still stirring, and cook until evenly blended and hot. Add the salt, pepper and nutmeg and cook a few minutes more. Reserve.

(continued)

ASSEMBLY

16 large cooked artichoke bottoms,
   heated
16 poached eggs   (see page 92)
hollandaise sauce   (see page 92)

Put equal amounts of creamed spinach on 8 plates. Place artichoke bottoms on top of the creamed spinach. Top with poached eggs and ladle hollandaise over each portion.

GRILLADES AND GRITS

SERVINGS: 8
PREPARATION TIME: 1 HOUR

¾ cup olive oil
 5 cloves garlic, finely chopped
 3 cups green pepper, chopped
 3 cups white onions, coarsely chopped
¾ cup celery, chopped
 1 bunch green onions, chopped
 8 ripe tomatoes, diced
2–3 teaspoons salt
about ½ teaspoon black pepper
 3 bay leaves, crushed
 2 quarts beef stock
 2 tablespoons Worcestershire sauce
 4 tablespoons cornstarch mixed
   with ½ cup water
 3 pounds beef or veal round
flour to dredge
½ cup butter
 4 cups freshly cooked grits

To prepare the sauce, heat the olive oil in a large heavy saucepan; add garlic, green pepper, white onion, celery, and green onions and brown. Add the tomatoes, salt, pepper and bay leaves and stir to mix thoroughly. Add the beef stock and the Worcestershire sauce and cook stirring and skimming frequently for about 5 minutes. Stir in the cornstarch mixed with water. Correct seasoning.

Pound the beef or veal rounds with the scored side of a mallet and, if necessary, cut into pieces about 5 × 5 inches. Dredge with flour, melt the butter in a heavy skillet and sauté the meat for about 6–8 minutes on each side until nicely browned.

Just before serving put the meat in the sauce to heat it through. To serve, spoon the sauce over the meat and serve the grits on the side.

Bananas Foster

SERVINGS: 4
PREPARATION TIME: 10 MINUTES

4 *tablespoons butter*
1 *cup brown sugar*
½ *teaspoon cinnamon*
4 *tablespoons banana liqueur*
4 *bananas, cut in half lengthwise, then halved*
¼ *cup dark rum, heated*
4 *scoops vanilla ice cream*

Melt the butter over an alcohol burner in a flambé pan. Add the sugar, cinnamon and banana liqueur and stir to mix. Heat for a few minutes, then place the halved bananas in the sauce and sauté until soft and slightly browned. Add the heated rum and flame. Lift the bananas carefully out of the pan and place four pieces over each portion of ice cream. Spoon the hot sauce over the bananas.

Note: This dish can also be prepared on top of the stove, then brought to the dinner table and flamed.

CHEF GERARD CROZIER
CROZIER'S

Gerard Crozier is a man of few words but the delicious aromas of mingling stocks enveloping his dining rooms say it all. The chef cooks. He doesn't believe in the tall white toque because it "doesn't do anything for the food" and he doesn't change his menu because he likes it the way it is.

"I have special dishes that I make every night, aside from the regular menu," Gerard says. "On Tuesdays I make braised rabbit in tomato sauce; with it I would serve an appetizer of Paté de Canard—marinated chicken livers, pork and veal cooked in white wine and brandy with fresh herbs. I bake it after lining the pan with pork fat. We serve a fresh vegetable and house salad with our entrées and a cheese platter or lemon tart would be good for dessert."

Gerard's low-keyed nonchalance about the food in his restaurant is rather typical of this young man from Lyon, where the food speaks louder than any words. His dishes are absolute simplicity, but the ingredients and Gerard's mastery of the food is what writers must mean when they speak of the great cuisine of Lyon. The Thursday night special, Filet Perigordine, is a blending of ingredients so basic that a heavy hand could ruin the magical sauce of glace de viand, cognac, and red wine, all reduced then thickened with a roux after which Gerard stirs goose liver paté into the sauce and spoons it over a tender filet of beef. He might make a leg of veal for Saturday, served with sautéed shrimp and a reduced sauce of cognac and whipping cream. He will definitely make a seafood terrine, grinding together shrimp and trout, adding cream, eggs, white wine, gelatin, and herbs and serve it in a smooth sauce of Dijon mustard, cream, seasonings and tarragon. Gerard's food is spare but filled with the flavors of the French chef.

Born in Lyon, Gerard had the usual apprenticeship in France at age 14 because, he says, "I did so poorly in school that I had to prepare for a profession." He spent two years in Lausanne as assistant to the chef of a seafood restaurant, then two years as sous chef in St. Tropez, followed by a series of jobs in French restaurants. In 1970, Gerard and his wife, Evaline, moved to Milkwaukee where he became a sous chef at a fancy private club. "It was very difficult," says Gerard. "I didn't speak English and no one in the kitchen spoke French. So I had to go to school and learn the language."

Gerard left the kitchen for eight years to concentrate on administrative work for the Royal Sonesta chain of hotels in Key Biscayne and New Orleans. In 1977, Gerard and Evaline opened their first restaurant in a shopping center in New Orleans East,

where he could be his own chef.

The present restaurant, built in 1979, is in the same district, a small, provincial-type building with a compact kitchen and seventeen tables, serving sixty-five diners. "I keep it small because my customers like to see me walking through the dining rooms; they can talk to me and I know what they like to eat. I serve only French wines; my regular guests know what is on the menu and when I serve the specials."

The menu is spare but those delicious stocks simmering on the back of the stove tell the whole story. Crozier's deserves its reputation and Gerard should stay in his kitchen, keeping his menu simple and the dishes sublime. ⚡

CROZIER'S
NEW ORLEANS

MENU

SEA SCALLOP APPETIZER
Sautéed scallops accompanied by a mustard sauce

ASPARAGUS WITH HOMEMADE MAYONNAISE
Cooked asparagus topped with a smooth hand-beaten dressing

CHICKEN IN CREAM SAUCE
Roast chicken served with rice pilaf

CRÈME CARAMEL
Individual cups of egg custard with caramel coated bottoms

✗

SERVINGS: 4–6
PREPARATION TIME: 20 MINUTES

2 egg yolks
2 teaspoons Dijon mustard
salt and white pepper to taste
2 cups peanut oil
1 tablespoon red wine vinegar, heated
1 teaspoon Worcestershire sauce
Tabasco to taste
1 tablespoon parsley, chopped
1 tablespoon tarragon leaves, chopped
2 tablespoons tomato paste
2 pounds scallops
1 teaspoon tarragon leaves, chopped
¼ cup butter

Blend egg yolks, mustard, salt and white pepper in a bowl. Gradually whisk the oil into this mixture. When thick, whisk in hot vinegar, Worcestershire sauce, Tabasco, parsley, tarragon and tomato paste.

Melt butter in a sauté pan. Sprinkle scallops with 1 teaspoon chopped tarragon, salt and pepper. Sauté scallops in butter for about 3 minutes, until they turn opaque.

Arrange scallops on a bed of lettuce on small plates. Spoon sauce on the side and garnish with fresh chopped parsley if desired.

SERVINGS: 4
PREPARATION TIME: 30 MINUTES

3 teaspoons Dijon mustard
2 egg yolks
salt and white pepper to taste
2 cups peanut oil
2 teaspoons red wine vinegar, heated
4 dozen asparagus

In a bowl blend mustard, egg yolks, salt and pepper. Gradually whisk oil into egg yolk mixture. When thick, add the hot vinegar to the mixture whisking constantly until smooth. Peel asparagus 3 inches from the top to the bottom of the stem. Cook in boiling salted water uncovered for 7–10 minutes until tender. Plunge into ice water to cool, then drain on a cloth. To serve, arrange the asparagus on small plates and spoon mayonnaise on top. Sprinkle chopped parsley on top if desired.

Chicken in Cream Sauce

CHICKEN IN CREAM SAUCE

SERVINGS: 4
PREPARATION TIME: 35 MINUTES

CHICKEN AND CREAM SAUCE
- 2 *chickens cut into serving pieces*
- 2 *tablespoons oil*
- 1 *tablespoon butter*
- ¼ *cup white wine*
- 2 *cups cream*
- salt and white pepper to taste

Note: ½ pound mushrooms may be added if desired.

Brown the chicken pieces on both sides, skin side first, in the heated butter and oil. Add salt and pepper. Transfer chicken to a 350-degree oven and bake about 15–20 minutes. Remove chicken from pan and keep warm. Pour off the grease and deglaze the pan with the white wine. Reduce wine by half and add the cream. Reduce until thick and correct seasonings. Heat chicken in sauce and serve with rice pilaf. Garnish with fresh chopped parsley if desired.

RICE PILAF

1/3 cup onion, chopped
2 tablespoons butter
1 bay leaf
2 cups raw rice
3 cups chicken stock, heated to boiling

Sauté the onions in butter with the bay leaf until the onions are transparent. Add the rice and toss to coat. Add the hot stock and bring to a boil. Put the pan in a 400-degree oven for 17–18 minutes. Fluff with a fork before serving.

SERVINGS: 15 1/2-CUP SERVINGS
PREPARATION TIME: 1 HOUR

CRÈME CARAMEL

CARAMEL
1/2 cup sugar
1/4 cup water

Bring sugar and water to a boil in a heavy pan, stirring to dissolve sugar. Let boil slowly until it turns the color of maple syrup and makes a thick caramel.

CUSTARD
4 cups milk
1/2 teaspoon vanilla
6 eggs
1 egg yolk
1 cup sugar

Scald the milk with the vanilla. Beat the eggs and egg yolk with the sugar until the mixture is thick and lemon colored. Pour on the scalded milk and beat vigorously until slightly cooled. Strain the custard.

ASSEMBLY

Pour the caramel into custard cups. Add strained custard. Put cups into a baking dish and add water halfway up the sides of the cups. Bake in a 350-degree oven for 35–40 minutes. Insert a knife near the edge of the cup to test for doneness. (If the knife comes out clean the custard is done.) Another test is to shake a cup. If the custard trembles it has not completely set. This dessert can be served warm or cold, unmolded or in cups.

Left to right: Booby Floyd, trombone; Freddie Kohlman, drums; Danny Rubio, tuba; Phamous Lambert, piano; Mike Sizer, clarinet; and Frank Trapani, trumpet.

Food and music are synonymous with New Orleans, where the Great Chefs series originated, so naturally each of the Great Chefs shows opens and closes with Dixieland jazz. The world-famous Dukes of Dixieland have been a New Orleans establishment since 1949. Like the first Great Chefs of New Orleans and the San Francisco series, their versatility and innate musicianship is such that they have included non-Dixieland music as well throughout the Great Chefs series.

The Dukes remain today one of the best proponents of New Orleans jazz. They perform nightly in their French Quarter nightclub, "Dukes' Place." In the course of a year they present sixty concerts, appearing with major symphonies and festivals in the great concert halls of the world, as well as one record album and at least one television musical.

In the past two decades, guitarist Charlie Byrd has emerged as a giant on the international music scene. Working with equal ease in both classical music and jazz, Byrd and his trio, as in the San Francisco television series, have added their special flavor to the More Great Chefs of New Orleans series. The technical proficiency derived from his classical training has opened up a new level of performance for Charlie Byrd—jazz played on a classical guitar without a pick or amplification.

Following a distinguished career studded with many honors, in 1980 Byrd and a group of his friends opened "Charlie's," a beautiful jazz and supper club in Georgetown, D.C. He continues to spend a portion of each year on the road, bring out new recordings, and write scores for films, television, modern dance and theatre.

ACKNOWLEDGEMENTS

🤸

PUBLISHER	AVON BOOKS THE HEARST CORPORATION
PROPRIETORS	WYES-TV, NEW ORLEANS TELE-RECORD PRODUCTIONS, LTD. 　NEW ORLEANS

BOOK PRODUCTION

EDITORIAL AND PRODUCTION SERVICES	JACK JENNINGS AND CYNTHIA MAYER BMR, SAN FRANCISCO
WRITER	NATALIE SCHRAM
RECIPE EDITOR	TERRI HINRICHS
DESIGN	MICHAEL PATRICK CRONAN
CALLIGRAPHY	GEORGIA DEAVER
PHOTOGRAPHY	JOE BERGERON DONALD MILLER CLIFF ROLAND
PUBLIC RELATIONS	LINDA NIX SALLY SHEPARD CANDICE JACOBSON

TELEVISION PRODUCTION

WYES-TV, NEW ORLEANS

TELEVISION PRODUCER AND WRITER	JOHN BEYER
ASSOCIATE PRODUCER	TERRI HINRICHS
NARRATORS	MARY LOU CONROY ANDRES CALANDRIA
LIGHTING	DAVE LANDRY
CAMERA	PAUL COMBEL
FIELD ENGINEER	DON SEARS
VIDEO EFFECTS	JIM MORIARTY
VIDEOTAPE EDITOR	JULIUS EVANS
ENGINEERING	SCOTT SCHEEL C. CALDWELL SAINZ STEVE HOWELL

TELE-RECORD PRODUCTIONS, LTD.

EXECUTIVE PRODUCER	JOHN SHOUP
MUSIC	CHARLIE BYRD TRIO THE DUKES OF DIXIELAND

REORDER FORM
(Please print)

☐ YES, I wish to order _____ additional copies of New Orleans II cookbooks at $9.95 each, plus $2.95 shipping and handling.

☐ YES, I wish to order _____ additional San Francisco cookbooks at $9.95 each, plus $2.95 shipping and handling.

☐ YES, I wish to order _____ additional copies of New Orleans I cookbooks at $9.95 each, plus $2.95 shipping and handling.

☐ YES, I am interested in additional information on Great Chefs of:

New Orleans
_____ videocassettes
_____ aprons
_____ calendars
_____ coffee cups
_____ posters

San Francisco
_____ videocassettes
_____ aprons
_____ calendars
_____ coffee cups

TOTAL for my order is $_____

_____ My check or money order is enclosed.

_____ Charge my credit card account.

_____ Visa   _____ Master Card   _____ Amex   _____ Diners

Account # _____ Expiration date _____

Signature _____

_____ Please send further information.

_____ Please send my gift order to the name and address I have provided.

Gift recipient: _____

_____

My name _____ Street _____

City _____ State _____ Zip code _____

PLEASE ALLOW FOUR WEEKS FOR DELIVERY

✄

GREAT CHEFS, P.O. BOX 71112,
NEW ORLEANS, LA 70172-9990